EVERYDAY LIFE IS A SERMON

Life with God's Word

God is speaking to you daily.
Are you listening?

Sierra Dunklin

ISBN 978-1-0980-8613-8 (paperback)
ISBN 978-1-0980-8614-5 (digital)

Christian Faith Publishing, Inc.
832 Park Avenue
Meadville, PA 16335
www.christianfaithpublishing.com

Printed in the United States of America

To those who are struggling to hear the voice of God, especially in those seasons of life where God feels so far away, I pray the stories in this book show you that God is working in our lives even when it seems He is moving silently. I pray that the scriptures that I used from the King James version of the Bible are thought-provoking and do what the Word is intended to do: break the yokes from your life and stir up the joy of the Lord.

> And behold the lord passed by, and a great and strong wind rent the mountains, and brake in pieces the rocks before the Lord; but the lord was not in the wind: and after the wind an earthquake; but the Lord was not in the earthquake: And after the earthquake a fire; but the Lord was not in the fire; but after the fire a still small voice. (1Kings 19:11–12)

Sometimes we miss God searching for the spectacular.

CONTENTS

ACKNOWLEDGMENTS

———— ✺ ————

I want to thank God who is the head of my life, the Author and Finisher of my faith. I thank God for His Son Jesus who died on the cross and raise on the third day, washing my sins way. I thank God for the Holy Spirit in which I can do all things through Christ who strengthens me.

I want to thank my sisters Alnesha and Angelica for always being a listening ear and encouraging me to go after my dream. I want to thank my mom for encouraging my writing skills by buying me journals THROUGHOUT MY LIFE and providing me an environment where I can live out my dreams. I want to thank my nieces Maya and Madison for just being alive; they are truly God's gift to me. THEIR CHILDLIKE FAITH IS INSPIRING. I PRAY ME STEPPING OUT IN FAITH ENCOURAGE THEM TO BELIEVE THAT GOD CAN DO WHAT THEY BELIEVE TO BE IMPOSSIBLE.

DAY 1

———— ❧ ————

Stay Connected!

For I know the thoughts that I think towards you, saith the Lord,
thoughts of peace and not evil, to give you an expected end.
—Jeremiah 29:11

PRELUDE

The beginning of moving forward towards my dream—a mini sermon for a class inspired me to look for God in my day-to-day life
for thirty days, allowing every event of my personal life to be connected with the Word of God. In addition, the women's conference
I attended stirred something in me. I have always wanted to write a
book. This felt like a good time to act on faith. The Bible says if we
draw near to God, He will draw closer to us. I felt as if I was going
through a dry spell in my life. I believe God was with me, but I was
having a hard time hearing from Him. Was I too distracted with the
events going on around me? Whatever it was, I knew I should take
advantage of the world shutting down to draw near Him.

Now back to the message…

Currently, we are living in some foreign times. We are in a global
pandemic that has disrupted our normal lifestyle. We have strife and

division being broadcasted in the media, and we have our personal problems that we are going through. Nevertheless, God wants us to have an expected end. According to the *Strong's Concordance*, that word *expected* is *Tiqvah*, and it means "cord or attachment." The word *end* in Hebrew is *Achariyth*, and it means future. Although God's plan for us is of peace—which is *Shalom* meaning "prosperity, good health, etc."—the plans of God are not automatic. Whatever we connect ourselves to will determine the future we will have.

Let me share some context about Jeremiah 29. In the book of Jeremiah 29, we have the people of God being captured by the Babylonians and taken into a foreign land. While they were in that foreign land, God instructed them to do what I believe God is instructing us to do during these foreign times. God is instructing us to be fruitful and multiply, to work, get marry, and to pitch our tents in our new destination. God was not surprised by the condition of His people being captives, and He is not surprised by what is going on with you right now.

As followers of Jesus Christ, the Son of God, we understand that we are in a new covenant. Unlike in the old covenant where the people's sins were covered by the blood of sacrificial animals, the new covenant, through the blood of Jesus, washed our sins away so that anyone who receives Jesus as their Lord and Savior by confessing with their mouth and believing in their heart that God raised Jesus from the dead will be made a new creature, old ways have passed away. (1 Corinthians 5:17)

I want to share three action steps to help you stay connected with God during hard times. These three steps are not new, but sometimes, we need to be reminded about what we need to do to stay connected.

1) The first action step we can do to help us stay connected to God is *pray*. When we pray to God, we are communicating with Him. As we cast our cares upon Him, He hears us and gives us answers. The more time you spend with God, the more you will be able to trust Him at His Word. For example, in the natural, when you communicate with someone

on a daily basis, you begin to know them and trust them at their word.

2) The second action step we can do to help us stay connected to God is to *meditate on the word of God* in the Bible. The reason why the people in Jeremiah's time were able to listen to God was because they stayed connected to the Word of God through Jeremiah. Now, in the Old Testament, the people of God had prophets like Jeremiah, but we, in the new covenant, have the Word of God through Jesus, the Son of God. The word *meditate* in the Hebrew is *hagah*. It means to murmur, speak, ponder, or study. So study the Word of God, think on the Word of God, and speak the Word of God.

3) Lastly, to stay connected to God, you want to think on God. If God's thoughts toward us is of peace, then we should focus on peace. We have to protect the peace of God in our mind by guarding what we listen to and watch. For example, I have a sister who likes to watch crime shows. Every day, she would call me to talk about an episode she watched. There were some episodes I could listen to her talk about, but then there were some episodes I could not listen to. I would have to tell her to stop telling me the story. In social work, there is a model called the *Cognitive Triangle*. It illustrates what you think on determine how you feel and what you feel determine how you act.

If you focus on the things of the world, you will feel despair, fear, and worry which will lead you to try to figure things out instead of going to God.

However, if you focus on God being our *Provider, Strong Tower, Present Help*, and *all we need*, then we will have feelings of hope and confidence, and those feelings will cause us to trust God and obey Him.

One biblical account that comes to mind when focusing on what happen when we keep our mind on God is found in Matthew 14:29. Peter asked Jesus could he come to Him and Jesus responded "come." During the storm, Peter saw Jesus and began to walk on water to get to Him, but when Peter began to focus on the storm, he lost sight of God and began to sink. Thank God! He is always there to catch us when we fall. So let's do our part by staying connected to God and having a peaceful end.

What are you going through today? Remember you already have the victory. The greater one lives in you and is greater than he that is in the world. That means no matter what the world throws at you, you can overcome it. I know that it is a scary thought. You are probably thinking the worst scenario and wondering if Jesus is enough. I encourage you to first settle in your heart that God loves you, and the thoughts that He thinks toward you are of peace.

First John 4:4 states, "You are of God, little children, and have overcome them, because greater is He that is in you, than he that is in the world."

Philippians 4:13 states, "I can do all things through Christ who strengthens me." That word *strengthens* in the Greek is *endunamoo*. It means "to enable or make strong." The reason you can do all things through Christ is because He will enable you or make you strong to overcome the things that is meant to harm you.

Lastly, I submit this to you. Jeremiah 1:8 says, "Be not afraid of their faces: for I am with thee to deliver thee, saith the Lord." The Lord is with you; He will deliver you. Don't allow what you see to disconnect you from God. He is with you. He loves you.

Stay connected.

DAY 2

Know Your Position in Christ

And as the people were in expectation, and all men mused in their hearts of John, whether he were the Christ or not; John answered, saying unto them all, I indeed baptized you with water: but one mightier than I cometh, the latchet of whose shoes I am not worthy to unloose; He shall baptize you with the Holy Ghost and with fire.
—Luke 3:15–16

Not everyone is called to what the church calls the "five-fold ministry" to work in the church as an *apostle, pastor, teacher, evangelist,* and *prophet.* However, God may have you work outside the church in the world. Nevertheless, you should still know what God has called you to do to "edify the body of Christ." If you are a Christian, a follower of Christ, you are part of the body, and you have a purpose.

Do you know who and what God has called you to do and where He has called you to be? If you do not know, others will place titles on you and guide you to places you should not be.

First Corinthians 14:10 states, "There are, it may be, so many voices in the world and none of them is without significance." Do you know your place in Christ's body? Living in the world where the enemy speaks loudly, if you are not focused on God and what He wants you to do, it could be hard to hear or distinguish God's voice from other influences. There's peer pressure; there's lust of the eyes, media influences, riches, fame, etc. trying to fight for your attention and want to push their agenda on you.

Don't fall for the trap!

What may look or sound good maybe detrimental to your purpose; this means a good idea can take you off your God-given course. Of course, God has given us a choice: life and death, your way or God's way. There is a proverb that states "there is a way which seemeth right unto a man, but the end thereof are the ways of death" (Proverbs 14:12).

Do you know where God is calling you? If you are on a different path, are you willing to get on the right path with God?

I believed God was calling me into ministry at a young age. My sister and I would play church. I was the pastor; she was the congregation and the choir along with our stuffed animals. However, as I continued to live life, I allowed my talents to steer me instead of seeking God for directions. I wanted to help people; I was a good listener, and people would come to me for advice. That sounded like a therapist to me. However, I also wanted to travel the world and went to college for international business and ended up enrolling in social relations to focus on the domestic social problems in my country. After still trying to find out what I wanted to do without seeking God, I decided to do what I was good at, and that was therapy, thus I obtained a master's degree in social work.

I am so glad that God called me again into ministry in 2013 because if I was called in 2018, I would have thought my failure to pass the test motivated me to go to ministry. I wonder how life would have been if I just received what God placed in my heart as a child and moved in that direction?

Thank God our beginning does not determine our finished product. Anything can change in the middle of your story. According to Romans 8:28, "And we know all things work together for good to them that love God, to them who are called according to his purpose." If you feel that you are on the wrong path, submit yourself to God, and He will get you on the right path.

John the Baptist knew his role and did not allow the people to push him into a position he was not called to be in. Jonathan, the son of King Saul, accepted that David would be king and did not allow the traditions of the dynasty or his father to push him into a role he was not called to be in.

Know your position!

Whether you are called in the five-fold ministry or outside it, never forget that you are a member of the body of Christ. No matter what God has called you to do, do it with confidence, and trust Him. First Corinthians 12:18 states, "But now hath God set the members every one of them in the body as it hath pleased him." We are all called to preach the gospel of Christ, allowing our good works to glorify God. Everyone is important because it takes all of us to complete the mission of edifying or building the church.

DAY 3

A Dream Buried

*And they returned and prepared spices and ointments; rested
the sabbath day according to the commandment.*

—Luke 23:56

The Hebrew word for rest is *hesuchazo*; it means to keep still, hold peace, or be quiet.

What to do when it looks like your dream has died due to circumstances?

In Luke 23:56, the women disciples were preparing the oils to anoint Jesus's body, and then they rested. Even though Jesus was dead, the women kept on working on what they could, and when they completed all they could do, they rested.

When it seems like a dream has died because of circumstances, when you can't see pass the circumstances, do what you can, and when you have done all you could, rest. Be still; hold your peace, and be quiet.

I can imagine how the followers of Christ might have felt when they placed him in the tomb. They probably felt stuck, uncertain about the future. They knew what Jesus said: "The Son of man must suffer many things, and be rejected of the elders and chief priests and scribes, and be slain, and be raised the third day" (Luke 9:22). Yet the wait tested their trust in Jesus's words.

You are probably in a situation that might look different than the plan God gave you. You're probably wondering like, *I know what God called me to do; I know how the end should look, but the middle makes me wonder, How do I get from this point to the great future God told me about?* I want to encourage you to rest. When you have done all God has told you or showed you, but now you are at a standstill…REST!

The rest period is not the time to be anxious, not the time to try and make things happen, or even doubt. The rest period is a time to keep still, hold your peace, and be quiet. Do not allow your words to be a snare to God's plan for you.

You are a farmer… You have planted on good ground, and like the bishop at my church always say, "You plant the seed, then you go to bed, get up, and praise God!"

Here are a few scriptures on resting in God:

> Be still and know that I am God: I will be exalted among the heathen, I will be exalted in the earth. (Psalm 46:10)

> The Lord shall fight for you, and ye shall hold your peace. (Exodus 14:14)

Remember, in the waiting period, God is fighting for your victory. When Jesus was in the grave, He was fighting to give us victory. When Daniel was waiting twenty-one days, the angel Gabriel was fighting to give Daniel victory. The same is true today. In the spirit realm, God and His hosts are fighting for the manifestation of your victory!

> But whoso hearkenth unto me shall dwell safely and shall be quiet from fear of evil. (Proverbs 1:33)

When you rest, you will see your dreams come alive. Just like those women by the tomb, when they came to an end of their work, they rested, and the next day, they saw the manifestation of their hope through faith.

DAY 4

―――――― ❦ ――――――

Are You Too Self-Involved?

But he, wanting to justify himself, said to Jesus, "And who is my neighbor?" Then Jesus answered and said: "A certain man went down from Jerusalem to Jericho, and fell among thieves, who stripped him of his clothing, wounded him, and departed, leaving him half dead. Now by chance a certain priest came down that road. And when he saw him, he passed by on the other side. Likewise a Levite, when he arrived at the place, came and looked, and passed by on the other side. But a certain Samaritan, as he journeyed, came where he was. And when he saw him, he had compassion. So he went to him and bandaged his wounds, pouring on oil and wine; and he set him on his own animal, brought him to an inn, and took care of him. On the next day, when he departed, he took out two denarii, gave them to the innkeeper, and said to him, 'Take care of him; and whatever more you spend, when I come again, I will repay you.' So which of these three do you think was neighbor to him who fell among the thieves?" And he said, "He who showed mercy on him." Then Jesus said to him, "Go and do likewise."
—Luke 10:29–37 (NKJV)

The point I want to make from this scripture is…are you too self-involved to care for another, especially when you see them hurting? Jesus is telling a parable about a good Samaritan. He tells about a certain man who went down from Jerusalem to Jericho and was robbed by thieves. Down the road, where the injured man laid, three men saw him. The priest saw him and passed him by; the Levite saw him and passed him by. However, the Samaritan, the man without a title, saw him and had compassion on him.

There is always an opportunity to be a blessing to someone or something. However, if you're too involved with yourself, that can keep you from looking beyond yourself. For example, I was walking to work from the parking lot. As I was walking, I saw a bug on the ground on its back; because I was so focused on getting to work—although I had plenty of time to spare—I passed it by and prayed that the wind or someone would flip it off its back. Still focusing on self, I made it to work, and I saw a coworker by the elevator. I passed by her and got on the elevator. In the elevator, I wondered if she was trying to get on the elevator. This began to bother me: first, the insect and then the lady; I was becoming inconsiderate. I finally took my blazer off…to my surprise, a fish fly flew off my blazer to the window of my cubicle. I was going to kill it until I rehearsed the prior inconsiderate incidents. I decided to let it live.

It doesn't cost anything to be kind. It is better to give than to receive. It does not feel good whenever you are in a situation where you are becoming overwhelmed with your thoughts or life, so step outside of yourself, and do something for someone; it will make you feel good, and sometimes, helping others will help you.

I remember a time in 2014; my sister and I was driving down a dark street. As I was driving, I saw a dark shadow in the middle of the street. I turned my high beam on and noticed a man in the middle of the street looking disheveled. I looked to the ground and noticed chips on the ground. (You want to see the move of God? Try stepping outside of yourself and do something for someone else.) It looked like this person had been hit. I pulled over and asked him if he was okay. He sounded muffled. I called 911. I kept my lights on him and blocked him in a way to prevent him from getting hit by other cars. All of a sudden, Good Samaritans started coming onto the scene.

God will provide. There was a nurse that helped out; strangers were gathering together and working together to help this man who appeared to be hit by a car. We blocked the street off; someone provided blankets so the man could lay down. Finally, the ambulance appeared on the scene and picked the man up and took him to the hospital. A miracle was presented all because people decided to not pass by the stranger but help him. That happened years ago, and I still get joyous thinking about how God used everyone to save this man's life.

When you feel down, do something for someone who cannot pay you back. The reward is in the giving.

DAY 5

—— ❧ ——

Are You Missing Opportunities Waiting for the Spectacular?

Boast not thyself tomorrow; for thou knowest
not what a day may bring forth.

—Proverbs 27:1

Today, I had an opportunity to have an application installed on my work computer. However, I allowed the opportunity to slip because I was focused on starting the holiday early. The time was now; the environment was conducive for me to be a priority because majority of the staff called off work. Now I have to hope that the tech support will be able to fit me into their schedule when all the staff returns to work on Wednesday.

There is a proverb that states "the little foxes spoiled the vine." I also believe that small opportunities can lead to great success. There are times when we put off the little things not realizing the great impact it can cause in our lives. In church, the bishop will have an agenda but will allow the flow of the Holy Spirit to trump his agenda. We should be the same way in our daily lives yielding to be flexible when opportunities present itself outside of our plan.

I had a plan to leave early from work and even parked the car to where I would have shorter distance to travel once I left work early, yet I should have been willing to adjust my plans to allow this opportunity to maximize my productivity when I return to work on Wednesday. It is okay to have a plan each day; however, be flexible to adjust your plans when opportunities present itself to better you.

DAY 6

—— ❧ ——

Stop Limiting Yourself...
It's You He Wants!

*And he gave some, apostles; and some, prophets; and
some evangelist; and some pastors and teachers.*
—Ephesians 4:11

In a world where there are so many followers, you may at times want
to be the one being followed. How do you compete with what has
been done? There is nothing new under the sun. Perhaps, that's why
we have remake of movies and songs. However, sometimes, the issue
is not with the message but the delivery. That's when YOU come in!
God has a specific assignment for you. He needs you to get the message across, and your uniqueness is in the delivery.

There are times when God gives me something in my spirit to
do. Initially, I am excited, but when I focus on everyone else, I would
get discouraged. I would think, *Now maybe I heard wrong*, there are
too many people giving the same message. I failed to notice that
although we are given the same message, our delivery is different,
and that is what makes us special. The message is good, but how we
deliver it determines who will hear it.

God has given you a dream, and you may be hesitant to act
because you think it's been done before. LAY THOSE THOUGHTS ASIDE;
you are the special sauce. Go ahead and do what God has called you

to do. There are people who need your delivery for them to hear the message. The same way God called many ministers for the same message, He wants you to do your part. Stay in your lane.

DAY 7

—— ✑ ——

What Is Your Reputation?

A good name is rather to be chosen than great riches
and loving favor rather than silver and gold.

—Proverb 22:1

The Hebrew word for name is *Shem*. It means "an appellation as a mark on memorial of individuality."

Ecclesiastes 7:1 says, "A good name is better than precious ointment."

This morning, I was watching a musical play with my mom. In the play, the general said to this rising star, "Your reputation precedes you." Before, this general knew this person's face; he knew his name. In life, people will hear about you before they meet you. That is why what you do in secrecy or in small groups matter. Your name travels fast; thus, you are responsible for the reputation attached to your name. Of course, there are people who may lie on your name, but it is what you do that will determine if the rumors are true or false.

There are many people and products, and we invest in them because of their reputation. A good name can open doors for you. What individual mark are you creating in this world, in your family, community, or career? When people hear your name, how would they perceive you?

DAY 8

———— ✑ ————

Message Sent: Taking the Good with the Bad

Also, take no heed unto all words that are spoken;
lest thou hear they servants curse you.
—Ecclesiastic 7:21

If a person wants to be offended, they will be. Have you ever had a time when someone gave you advice you did not ask for? In communicating, sometimes a good message gets lost in the delivery. So pay attention to the message.

Today, I was volunteering, and one of the volunteers advised me on how to do my job. My initial feeling was offense. My thoughts, *No one asked you for help. Oh, so you think I don't know how to do my job, etc.* However, I smiled and thanked her and did my job. The message she gave me was not wrong, yet I found it to be offensive based on what I thought about her delivery (intrusive) and even my insecurities in my position.

If I would have succumbed to my emotions, I would have hindered the mission we were brought together to complete. Why cause problems? Perhaps today, I did not need her help, but how I responded could have prevented her from helping me in a time when I might need help. Whether in church, work, or any project that takes a group effort, the enemy will try to cause strife to prevent the mission from taking place. We, as the body of Christ, have to be vigilant and not give into Satan's tactics. Satan is subtle; therefore, we have to be on watch. Satan has not changed from when he was in the garden and tempted Adam and Eve.

He is no different than when he caused fear to enter the heart of the Pharaoh that he enslaved the Hebrews for being too many in the land (Exodus 1:8–11). He is no different than when he attempted to tempt Jesus, and he is the same today. Therefore, we should "forbear one another; and forgiving one another, if any man have a quarrel against any; even as Christ forgave you so also do ye" (Colossians 3:13).

When you think the best of others, you tend to think the best of their intentions.

Not everyone is out to get you.

DAY 9

Pleasant Principle

This is the day which the Lord hath made;
we will rejoice and be glad in it.

—Psalms 118:24

Don't miss the beauty of today seeking the spectacular.

Today was a good day. I simply enjoyed the simple things of life—things money can't buy and people tend to overlook. I spent time with my family. My younger cousins came over to play with my nieces. No one was injured, which is always a blessing when children get together. There was peace in my home, and I accomplished some things. Today was productive, and my face was healing from a sunburn, which developed a couple of days ago. Today was simple. Every day is a sermon even when the day is still. There is always a reason to glorify God.

With so much going on in the world, I am always blessed to see my nieces and younger family members not having their innocence robbed from them. I thank God that I can provide a safe environment for my younger family members not to have their innocence robbed from them. I thank God that I can provide a safe environment for my young family members to have fun and be children, even if it is in the backyard. Thank God for the backyard, for the space.

At the end of the day, your day, if you ever wonder if God is with you, just look around and count your blessings. During this

COVID-19 season, I experienced loss of smell and taste. I lost some of my hair, but I thank God that I am recovered. Thank God for your life. I used to get irritated when people would say, "Thank God you are alive," and I would retort, "Death must be better" (because things were not going my way). I was just ready to be with the Lord. That was until I had a near-death experience to where I was begging God to let me live. The beauty of waking up is the hope that you're getting closer to your heart's desire. God loves you, and He wants what is best for you. Stay with Him. Rejoice and be glad in today.

Today is the day that the Lord has made! Name five things you are thankful for in this day?

1) _____
2) _____
3) _____
4) _____
5) _____

DAY 10

———— ✿ ————

Put the Pen to the Paper

*And the Lord answered me and said Write the vision and
make it plain upon tables, that he may run that readeth.
For the vision is yet for an appointed time…*
—Habakkuk 2:2–3

I am excited about this book not only for the Word of God used to
break yokes in your situation but also because I can see the finished
product. I can finally see this project to completion.

The word *run* in Hebrew is *ruwts*. It means "to rush." In
Habakkuk, God was instructing the prophet Habakkuk to write the
vision down so that the readers could hold fast to the vision. When
you have a vision written down, you are able to either observe and
measure the distance you are at to get to the finish line or make some
adjustments before getting to the finish line.

Deuteronomy 6:6–9 shows the purpose and importance of having your vision before you:

> And these words, which I command thee
> this day, shall be in thine heart: And thou shalt
> teach them diligently unto thy children, and shalt
> talk of them when thou sittest in thine house,
> and when thou walkest by the way, and when
> thou liest down, and when thou risest up. And

thou shalt bind them for a sign upon thine hand, and they shall be as frontlets between thine eyes. And thou shalt write them upon the posts of thy house, and gates.

People tend to focus on the things that are in front of them.

Has God given you a vision for your future? How do you see yourself? Where do you see yourself? Don't let the vision get away. God's plan will always prevail; however, you get to choose if you will answer the call or ignore it. There's a story in the Bible in Judges 4 where God instructed Deborah, a prophetess leading Israel in wartime, to give Barak a command to lead Israel into victory. However, because of Barak's hesitation to act, the victory came from Deborah instead of Barak, who it was intended to.

> Now Deborah, a prophet, the wife of Lappidoth, was leading Israel at that time. She held court under the Palm of Deborah between Ramah and Bethel in the hill country of Ephraim, and the Israelites went up to her to have their disputes decided. She sent for Barak son of Abinoam from Kedesh in Naphtali and said to him, "The LORD, the God of Israel, commands you: 'Go, take with you ten thousand men of Naphtali and Zebulun and lead them up to Mount Tabor. I will lead Sisera, the commander of Jabin's army, with his chariots and his troops to the Kishon River and give him into your hands.'" Barak said to her, "If you go with me, I will go; but if you don't go with me, I won't go." "Certainly I will go with you," said Deborah. "But because of the course you are taking, the honor will not be yours, for the LORD will deliver Sisera into the hands of a woman." So Deborah went with Barak to Kedesh. (Judges 4:4–9)

I encourage you to rush to the vision. You probably see a future that is different than how your present time look. Don't hold your future hostage by not acting accordingly in the present. You may have questions regarding your finances, your relationships, or marital status. You may wonder how does a person who study the Word, know the Word, go to church, and pay tithes not be in a place of prosperity. Sometimes the answer is based on what you are doing in your present: cause and effect. Those things I mentioned above is to position you to be in the right place, but you can be in the right place, and your failure to act on whatever God has put in your heart to do can postpone your victory. So act fast!

It has been a desire to write a book since I was a teenager. Truth be told, I have written plenty of books, but I would stop during the work in the middle of the plan. Partial obedience is still disobedience. You have to see the goal from start to finish while leaning on God to lead you in the middle. Who knows where I could have been by now if I would have stayed the course? God revealed to me some things years ago about my heart's desire. He informed me that I could have been in high positions long ago, but I quit too soon.

I would quit on things before it had time to manifest. I would get distracted with what I want at that present moment and take myself off the path God had me on. Or I would be in the right place but would not take advantage of the opportunities given to me. I used to think just being in the right place would bring me good fortunes. I had to learn that being in the right place would position me to receive, but in order to get the goods, I would have to act.

Write your vision down. I'm sure as you read this page, something is stirring up in you. If you feel you have lost your dream, humble yourself and go to God for answers. He wants you to shine in this world. So keep your vision in the forefront of your face. Write it down. When you complete the vision, begin a new one!

DAY 11

—⁓—

Don't Rush to Speak, Just Breathe!

But sanctify the Lord God in your hearts: be ready always
to give an answer to every man that asketh you a reason
of the hope that is in you with meekness and fear...
—1 Peter 3:15

Today at work, someone asked a question about the Bible regarding an action and whether that action would lead to hell. Immediately, a slew of emotions flooded my body, especially offense and anxiousness. I was offended because I thought she was being facetious. It wasn't like she was telling a joke. It was her delivery. To me, it felt as if she was trying to debate the validity of the Bible, hence why I became anxious. I was anxious at the thought that I would have to defend the Bible and how she may respond.

My experience with people who bring up conversation that is familiar to me but publicly ask someone else was usually a bait for me to join in, in which I was not taking the bait. I prefer to be invited into a conversation. However, I prepared my response in case she decided to invite me to the conversation.

Thank God she did not invite me to the conversation because I was not ready. My emotional state would have caused me to overreact. Here was a person who knows I am a Christian; if I had allowed my emotions to show, I could have compromised my witness of

God's love. It is okay to not have an answer right now. It is okay to sleep on a matter before responding.

As I thought about her comment about the Bible, God reminded me that people are on different levels when it comes to getting to know Him. Therefore, I should always keep the focus on Jesus. When I thought about Jesus, I remembered her comment about whether her actions would cause her to go to hell. If I would have entered the conversation, my response would have been a scripture that focused on salvation since that appeared to be her concern. I would have quoted Romans 10:8–10,13 so she could understand how to avoid going to hell.

There are times we miss opportunities to witness because we are so consumed with our emotions. Perhaps she really wanted to know if killing bugs would send her to hell, or perhaps she was being flippant. We had just had a conversation about God a few days ago; perhaps she avoided me because she was not ready to really hear the answer. Anyway, what I learned from the situation is to keep the communication on Jesus.

> But what saith it? The word is nigh thee, even in thy mouth, and in thy heart: that is the word of faith, which we preach; That if thou shalt **confess with thy mouth** the Lord Jesus, and shalt **believe in thine heart** that God hath raised him from the dead, thou shalt be saved. For with the heart man believeth unto righteousness; and with the mouth confession is made unto salvation. For the scripture saith, Whosoever, believeth on him shall not be ashamed. For there is no difference between the Jew and the Greek: for the same Lord over all is rich unto all that call upon him. For whosoever shall call upon the name of the Lord shall be saved. (Romans 10:8–13)

DAY 12

—— ⌘ ——

Don't Live in Regret

If we confess our sins, He is faithful and just to forgive us our sins, and to cleanse us from all unrighteousness.
—1 John 1:9

The Greek word for sin is *hamartia*. It comes from the root word *hamartano* which means "to miss the mark, to err, to offend."

I want you to know that if you feel you have missed the mark with God or you have offended someone, tell God your offense, and He will forgive you. Since God is willing to forgive you, you should also forgive yourself. Let no one make you feel bad for what you have delivered to God. And if those thoughts of the past or even thoughts of the future try to come against you, do what the Word of God says, "Humble yourselves therefore under the mighty hand of God, that he may exalt you in due time: Casting all your care upon him; for He careth for you" (1 Peter 5:6–7).

Today, I am at work, and a flood of thoughts came to my mind about one of the last conversations I had with my cousin in July 2013. He invited me to celebrate his birthday on his block. The *thought* of being around young people prevented me from going. I am sure he celebrated his birthday plenty of times, but this time was different. He invited me, and I turned him down. Not realizing that it would be his last birthday he would ever invite me to. I regretted not going. Even if I could have done a quick visit, I wished I would have gone.

Whenever I rehearse the conversation in my mind, I want to feel pity. I want to feel sorrow, just to prove how apologetic I am and that if given the opportunity to do it again, I would choose differently.

Have you ever been in a situation where you wish you could have done a do-over? I'm sure all of us have been in situations that given the information we have now, we would choose to act differently. That is why it is so important not to have pride about tomorrow coming that we put off things to a future we do not know will come. Of course, it is important to plan; we plan because we have hope. However, there are certain situations that we cannot plan for because we do not know what tomorrow will bring. The death of my cousin taught me that tomorrow isn't promised. Even the Bible shows it in scriptures:

> Take therefore no thought for the morrow: for the morrow shall take thought for the things of itself. Sufficient unto the day is the evil thereof. (Matthew 6:34)

> Boast not thyself of tomorrow; for thou knowest not what a day may bring. (Proverbs 27:1)

> Go to now ye that say Today or tomorrow we will go into such as city, and continue there a year and buy and sell and get gain: Whereas ye know not what shall be on the morrow. For what is your life? It is a vapour, that appeareth for a little time, and then vanisheth away. For that ye ought to say, If the Lord will we shall live and do this or that. (James 3:13–15)

Today while at work, I fought back the tears, and the scriptures I have on this page provided me relief. There is nothing wrong with crying over a loved one, a heartbreak, missing someone or something. However, I understand how the devil works. If I would have continued to feel sorry for a situation I couldn't change, I would have become depressed. Hope is for the future, not the past. If I continued to focus on the past, I would become hopeless, and once I lose hope, what would be the point of living?

Satan comes to kill, steal, and destroy. July 2013 was a missed opportunity that I could either learn from and not make the same mistakes with other relatives, or I could allow it to keep me in bondage. I loved my cousin, and I missed him dearly. But God is still God, and God has a plan for me. I will see my cousin again, but I cannot get that moment again. Therefore, I choose to live knowing that my cousin is in my future, not in my past.

I encourage you to move forward even in your tears, even if you have to continually cast your thoughts or cares upon God. Move Forward! Do not live in regret. Your future is bright!

DAY 13

—◦ℒ℘◦—

Beauty for Ashes

But as for you, ye thought evil against me; but God meant it unto good, to bring to pass as it is this day to save much people alive.
—*Genesis 50:20*

Let me first say that it is not my intention to make light of the pandemic. I am aware that there are some who have experienced great tragedy and loss because of this virus. My heart is with you. I pray that God strengthens you for the life ahead of you. I pray you feel God's love and comfort during this season, and know that despite what Satan did, God is greater, and He has a great future ahead of you.

I am also aware that this pandemic has been a blessing to some. I have heard of increased wealth, checks in the mail, a greater revelation of who God is, miracles occurring, etc.

Problems at Work

As for me, this has been a season where closet prayers have manifested openly. I appreciate everything God does in my life, whether it looks small or great. I have been working since May, and today I recognized something that I did not notice before. I was just thinking about how God answered my prayers but not in the way I thought it would happen. At work, I've been wanting to move my seat to a different location because the coworker behind me is a loud eater. Now to some of you, that may seem petty, but for me, hearing the smacking sounds of someone eating or popping their gum is torturous.

I battled about moving my seat because the person is nice, and I did not want her to be offended. I also did not want to lose my scenery, but I just could not take it anymore. I would pray to God every time she ate, and the days she was not at work, it was a blessing for me. Then the pandemic happened. I was able to be at home, and when we returned to work, my desk was at the location where I was going to ask my supervisor to place me. Is the location better than my former seating arrangement? It depends on what you value most: peace or scenery?

Another Closet Prayer Answered

Since God called me to evangelize in 2013, I have been stirred up and wanting to talk about God in sermons. Currently, I serve at my church's outreach department street-evangelizing team. I have been serving in this department for six years, and after watching my leaders preach a good word, I aspired to do the same. I have been delivered from my fear of speaking in front of people, and God has been speaking to me about some things I believe people could benefit from hearing. So in our January meeting, I was informed that this year could be the year where I encourage the team members with a word from God. I was excited. Then the pandemic hit, and the state of emergency ordered for the church to temporarily close down, and outreach was temporarily cancelled.

Do you think that stopped God? No! God was still preparing me to minister in front of a group. Thank God for technology. Even though the outreach was cancelled and it appeared the plans spoken of in January was delayed, I had the opportunity to minister the Word of God through Zoom!

In John 10:10, the Bible says Satan comes to kill, steal and destroy. When this pandemic hit, it was clear that its mission was to kill, steal, and destroy. However, when you focus on facts and not truths or you just hear one side of the story, you fail to see that when you keep reading in "verse 10," Jesus says, "I am come that they might have life, and that they might have it more abundantly" (John 10:10).

The facts are…we are in a global pandemic, and this virus has done some horrific things. Facts. Prayerfully, by the time you read this book, we are out of the pandemic. But if you are facing another negative chain of events, the truth does not change. The truth is, Jesus is alive, and if you will allow Him, He will give you beauty for ashes, the oil of joy for mourning, the garment of praise for the spirit of heaviness; for your shame, He will give you double honor. He will heal your broken heart, preach deliverance to the captives, recover the sight of the blind, and set free the abused (Isiah 61:1–11; Luke 4:18).

Cease the opportunity despite how it looks.

For me, my "ceasing the moment" is me finally writing a book God placed in my spirit to write years ago. **What do you have time to do?**

If you had more time, what would you do?

1) _____
2) _____
3) _____

Now listen! We are talking about your livelihood, your purpose in life. What would you need to do to make time? Start rearranging your life now.

1) _____
2) _____
3) _____

DAY 14

———— ❧ ————

My Breaking Point

There cometh a woman of Samaria to draw water: Jesus saith
unto her, Give me to drink. [For his disciples were gone away unto
the city to buy meat]. Then saith the woman to him, How is it
that thou, being a Jew askest drink of me, which am a woman
of Samaria? For the Jews have no dealing with the Samaritans,
Jesus answered and said unto her, If thou knewest the gift of God,
and who it is that saith to thee, Give me to drink; thou wouldest
have asked of him, and he would have given thee living waters.
—John 4:7–10

Has there ever been a time someone asked you to do something and
you questioned their motives? Better yet, have God asked you to
do something or give something and you hesitated because of your
insecurities? You think, *How is it you asked me to give? They have more*
than me; they are more _____ *than me* (fill in the blank).

In this scripture, here is a woman who is allowing her past experience or even the tradition in her community question what God
has asked her to do. Jesus asked her to do something that was in her
ability to do, and yet she hesitated. How many of us has God called
to do something, but we allow what people have said about us or
even the traditions of our community prevent us from stepping out
in faith? God was positioning her to receive something that would
edify her life. God does not need anything from us. The heaven is

41

His throne, and the earth is His footstool. When God calls us to do something, it is because He has greater for us.

The beauty of God is that He will never ask us to give what we don't have. He asked her for water, and she had the tools to do exactly what He had asked her. Yet we disqualify ourselves from the mission when we fail to see that if God has called us to do something, that means He will also qualify us to do it.

I titled this message "My Breaking Point" to encourage myself to stay the course. As the days go by, I am getting tired. Not tired of the lessons God has given me because my daily life consists of writing in my journals, talking to God, and talking to my sister about how good God is, and what He has shown me in His Word; however, it is different when documenting my experience. It's no fun when it becomes work.

Nevertheless, in my commitment to document every day, I have to fight back thoughts that were telling me to give up. Thoughts on what I am doing being done before and even doubts that God is calling me to write this book from past experience of people not valuing what I have to say. My thought was *"why write a book?"*

God will qualify the call on your life and my life if we trust Him at His word.

God will never ask you to do something He is not able to strengthen you to complete. When God placed in my spirit to write a book, He knew I could do it. And if I was willing to see this project to completion, He was able to empower me and make me strong enough to complete it.

What has God asked you to do that you feel you cannot do? (Fill in the blank.) _____

Let's set the record straight. You can do all things through Christ because God enables you and empowers you to do what He has called you to do.

The real question is, Do you want to do what God has placed in your heart to complete?

Do you? _____.

Do you understand how much God wants to bless you? God is not asking you to give what He is not willing to multiply. Jesus said to the Samaritan woman, "If you knowest the gift of God and who it is that saith to thee, Give me to drink; thou wouldest have asked of him and he would have given thee living water."

Don't hesitate! God is giving you something that could change your life. He has chosen you and equipped you to do what he has asked you to do.

Be blessed.

DAY 15

Check Your Thought

*Finally, brethren, whatsoever things are true, whatsoever things
are honest, whatsoever things are just, whatsoever things are pure,
whatsoever things are lovely, whatsoever things are of good report; if
there be any virtue, and if there be any praise, think on these things.*
—Philippians 4:8

In social work, there is a model called the Cognitive Triangle of Life.
Basically, what this triangle illustrates is that whatever you think on
will affect your mood, then your actions will correspond to how you
are feeling.

Today started off good. I woke up; I prayed. I wrote in my journal. I made plans to volunteer to serve at church. There was enough
gas to get me to church without stopping. Life is starting on a good
note.

Once I arrived at church and happy to serve, my mood changed.
At my church, because of the pandemic we are in, they conduct temperature screening because of the virus. Now it has been for about a
couple of weeks I have been screened at church. I get my temperature
taken, then I go serve. However, this time, I got my temperature
taken, and the person checking my temperature informed me that
my temp reading was 98 degrees. All of a sudden, my mind began
to wonder. I was able to pass through, yet my thoughts started rac-
ing: *Why did he tell me my temperature; was it a warning. Should I*

be concerned? Oh my! it is feeling hot in here; oh my, what if I get it? What if I affect someone else, etc., etc.? So even though I felt fine on my way to church and I was able to pass through, which indicated my temperature was not a concern, my thoughts were causing me to feel weighed down.

In this season, I am especially aware of the traumatic effects this pandemic has had on me emotionally and physically. Because of what I have experienced or even witnessed, sometimes I find myself being hypervigilant or even avoiding things to prevent me from reliving the trauma.

Have you ever had a traumatic experience that you survived, yet the thought brings you back to that place of trauma? You have survived, yet something unrelated can trigger you. Nevertheless, you have to keep living.

In Philippians 4:8, Paul is in prison and is writing to the church in Philippi encouraging them to keep a good attitude so they could live a peaceable life. Our thought life controls how we operate in the world. That is why it is so important to know God for yourself. When negative thoughts try to discourage you from living out your best life, remind yourself who God is. GOD IS LOVE. GOD IS PROVIDER. GOD IS PROTECTOR. GOD IS OUR HELP, etc. When God is elevated, the problem will cease.

No matter how great or small the problem is, put God first in your thoughts, and He will bring you peace. I was able to serve effectively because I focused on God. Satan comes to bring delusions. When you know that God has delivered you from a traumatic situation, do not allow your thoughts to hold you captive. Keep your mind on things that are edifying to your soul. Keep your mind on God.

DAY 16

Standing in the Gap

And I sought for a man among them, that should make
up the hedge, and stand in the gap before me for the land,
that I should not destroy it: but I found none.
—Ezekiel 22:30

As of late, my days have been good. I'm not sure if it is because I am more aware of my days or what. If I would have written this book in March, most of the sermons would have been on faith, healing, and trusting God. This book is to show how God speaks to us every day, so the scriptures reflected in this book are based on the events that occurred throughout the summer months.

The lesson I learned today was that our blessings are tied into another person's obedience, which could explain the delay. God's work will be done, and He will give you the opportunity to be blessed through your obedience, but if you refuse to do the work, then God will find someone else to do the job.

Yesterday, while cleaning my room, I found a check for $30. I was so excited because I planned to use that money for parking this week which was $30. In the middle of the day, I gave my sister $20 to buy some materials for my niece's celebration. In my mind, I'm thinking about how I needed that money for parking. My sister came back with the $20 saying that she decided to use her money. Thank the Lord! Then we went to the store so I could buy a birthday card for my niece. I decided to buy two birthday cards because my other niece's birthday was coming up next week.

However, once I decided which card to give my niece whose birthday we are celebrating, the Holy Spirit instructed me to give the other card to my cousin and put money in it. Initially, I negotiated because I was trying to hold on to my $20. Nevertheless, I obeyed God. Later in the day, I understood why God wanted me to give her the money.

While the children were hitting the piñata, it was my younger cousin's turn to hit the piñata. She almost cracked open the piñata after her attempts of hitting the piñata. Unfortunately, her turn was up, and the other person won the money. See, God sees all before it happens, and He makes provision for us in our time of need or want. If I did not prepare that money earlier, I highly doubt I would have given my cousin $20 just to make her feel better. No, it was my obedience earlier that made God able to use me to replace the money my cousin thought she lost in the game.

Have God instructed you to do something and you procrastinated on it? You may not understand how your obedience can be a blessing to someone's else life or how another person's obedience can benefit our life, but when God tells you to do something, do it. It may not make sense to you in the beginning, but do it.

This reminds me of an event in 1 Kings 17 where a prophet named Elijah was sent by God to Zarephath to see a widow woman to give him something to eat. The widow and her son were on their last meal. When Elijah asked the woman for food, of course, she was offended. At that moment, she could have refused because of her situation. Nevertheless, she yielded to the man of God, and in return, she was blessed.

God is in control. If He has commanded you to give out of what you have, trust Him. God is not poor, and He is known to give us double for our portion if we are obedient.

DAY 17

Now Faith

*Now Faith, is the substance for things hoped
for, the evidence of things not seen.*
—Hebrew 11:1

Ever been in a situation where you are looking for opportunities to
show the goodness of God?

Since I have been documenting my daily life, I have noticed that
I have missed a lot of opportunities to bless someone either because
I did not recognize the opportunity or it was not set up in a way that
I wanted to respond to. However, this time, I was not going to miss
the mark, in which I almost missed the mark.

So while at the party, my cousin complained about her back.
She asked if anyone knew what to do for back pain. Everyone was
giving their solution based on their knowledge and experience. I even
demonstrated my solution on the ground. Then I heard a still voice
saying, *lay your hand on her back.* It was like God was saying get off
that ground and use your faith for healing. So I got off the ground
and said I know what will work. I placed my hand on her back,
prayed in Jesus's name for healing, and we both said amen, which
means "so be it." I don't know if she noticed, but she stopped com-
plaining about her back.

I almost missed the opportunity because my mind was on
worldly solutions. I'm not saying that anything is wrong with med-

icine or whatnot. However, when someone is in need, it's best to let God be the first option. I have learned to call on the name of the Lord as a first option. Now if for whatever reason He decides to provide my healing through science, I am okay with that too; the objective is to be healed and allow God to navigate how He will decide to heal. Whether it is through the manifestation of healing with the laying on of hands or through doctors, people trained in the field, I am okay with it.

DAY 18

— ✺ —

Activating Your Faith

And believers were the more added to the Lord, multitudes both of men and women. Insomuch that they brought forth the sick into the streets, and laid them on beds and couches, that at the least the shadow of Peter passing by might overshadow some of them. Crowds gathered also from the towns around Jerusalem, bringing their sick and those tormented by impure spirits, and all of them were healed.

—Acts 5:14–16

I have been serving in my church's outreach department for six years, and I have never experienced a time, such as this, where we are not able to do outdoor ministry because being in contact with someone could be deadly. We are currently in a pandemic, and I pray that by the time this book comes out, the world would be in a post-pandemic age. Since March 2020, I have been sending monthly text to my group just checking on them. In my prayers, I have discussed my feelings about the state we are in with God, wondering if we would actually end the year with no outreach ministry.

Then today, I got a call from one of the leaders inquiring if I would be willing to serve outreach in August 2020. I listened, and I responded, "Yes, by faith." Meaning, it seems like a good idea to go out, but I haven't prayed on it to see if I should go. Typically, I follow the peace of the Holy Spirit that dwells in me. When I said yes, I felt peace because it has been something I have been praying to God about in my prayer time. I could not see any reason not to say yes.

Presently, we have people gathering together to protest, gathering together for parties. Are the people of God who carries the infilling of the Holy Spirit supposed to sit in the background while others make their mark in the world? No! We have what the world needs. If we can gather together to protest, gather together to party, why not gather together to introduce people to Jesus so that they get saved and be filled with the Holy Spirit? The time is now to show the world that God is alive, and He is working in the earth through His people. Glory to God!

When I hung up the phone from the leader of the outreach team, I began to build myself up: *Lord, if it is your will that we go out in the community to minister your word, I trust that you will also give us victory over COVID-19. You are greater than he that is in the world. Now has come the time for me to get off the sidelines and get into the game.* I don't know what will happen in August. I trust God. Proverbs 21:31 says, "The horse is prepared against the day of battle: but safety is of the LORD." I inquired about protective measures; he reported that we will have masks and gloves. As the proverb stated, we are prepared to go out, but safety is of the Lord. I trust that God would deliver.

I'm not nervous. I believe that the same power that Peter had when he walked passed the people and they were healed is the same Holy Spirit that dwells in us and our team (Acts 5:15). It's kind of exciting to live in a time where God would use us through the power of the Holy Spirit to heal all those we encounter. Many times we want to see the glory of God, yet we failed to operate in faith.

You, the readers, would have to catch the sequel to see what happened in August.

DAY 19

❧

Peer Pressure

And the Lord God said unto the woman, what is this that thou hast done? And the woman said, the serpent beguiled me, and I did eat.
—Genesis 3:13

How many of us have experienced making moves in life to prevent people from talking about us only to have our results give people something to talk about?

In this scripture, Eve is now explaining to God why she disobeyed His commandment to not eat from the tree of good and evil (I encourage you to read the whole chapter for clarity). People tend to display lack of sympathy for Eve's actions, but I, through life, have developed empathy for Eve. God commanded Adam and Eve not to eat of the tree of good and evil. However, when Satan came attempting to discredit God, Eve started doubting what she knew from God. When you read Eve's conversation with Satan, you will see that there was no misunderstanding on Eve's part when it came to God's commandment of her. However, because she entertained what Satan said, she began to plant doubt in her mind and eventually talked herself into doing what was wrong in God's eyes.

How many of us will admit to doing what we know to be wrong, yet we do it because it provides a reward to us? Now, I know the example that I am going to give is minuscule; however, the point I want to make is, the pressure to respond based on how a person may perceive you can have you doing things that may result in you having resentment for your behavior or even embarrassment.

Each day is a work in progress for me. There are times when I am confident, especially when I know what I know, and there are times where I struggle, and I allow what people will think of me cause me to act out of my emotions versus what I know. I pray that I will get to the point where I am comfortable in my skin to where the thoughts of people are not cumbersome to me. However, because of past experiences, I tend to find myself trying to not do what caused me to be ridiculed by others. It seems smart to not behave in a way that caused people to mock you such as cutting in line, interrupting someone's conversation, or offering advice without the person's permission.

Nevertheless, there are times when a person will peer pressure you or even encourage you to respond in a way that is not beneficial for you yet rewarding for them—such as someone wanting you to speed up because they think driving the speed limit is slow, setting you up on a date so they could get closer to a particular person, or encouraging you to drink or do drugs because it gives them something to talk about later. The latter examples may cause people to ridicule you, but to participate in those activities could cause greater consequences to you if you yield to it. There must be balance.

The circumstance I am using is based on how I felt peer pressured to respond in a way that could have caused a negative consequence for me. As I was leaving the church parking lot, I stopped at the red light. At first, I was waiting patiently for the light to turn green. Then I started to notice the cars on my left turning left to leave the parking lot while the light was red. I became anxious and began to question myself: *Can I too make this right turn while the light is red? Is this one of the situations where if the road is clear I can turn?* Then I noticed the cars behind me, and I became even more anxious. I would hate for someone to blow their horn at me *in the church parking lot.* Then I started rationalizing why I should turn. *The street in front of me is two-way; ahead of me is open land. I don't see any cars coming from the left or right? This turn should be okay. What if the person behind me have to go somewhere and I am holding them up?*

I decided to make the turn. Once I made the turn, I wondered if I just made an illegal turn. In my attempt to prevent the cars behind me from talking about me, I probably just gave them something to talk about.

> For what I am doing, I do not understand. For what I will to do, that I do not practice; but what I hate, that I do. If, then, I do what I will not to do, I agree with the law that it is good. But now, it is no longer I who do it, but sin that dwells in me. For I know that in me [that is, in my flesh] nothing good dwells; for to will is present with me, but how to perform what is good I do not find. For the good that I will to do, I do not do; but the evil I will not to do, that I practice. Now if I do what I will not to do, it is no longer I who do it, but sin that dwells in me. (Romans 7:15–20 NKJV)

Paul is making a statement on how he does what he does not want to do but do not do what he wants to do. However, it is his flesh that caused him to do the things that he does not want to do. The word *flesh* in the Greek is *sarx*. There are several definitions for the word *sarx*; however, the definition that I will focus on is human nature or human mindedness. Because of Paul's human nature, he warred within himself regarding doing what is right and refraining from what's wrong.

Thank God, Romans 8:1 states, "There is therefore now no condemnation to them which are in Christ Jesus, who walk not after the flesh but after the Spirit." When Eve disobeyed God, in the book of Genesis 3, she allowed entertaining Satan to rob her from her holy nature. When she and Adam ate of the tree of good and evil, they exchanged their holy nature for a fleshly nature where they operated from their soul (mind, will, and emotions) instead of their faith in God. We experience those same feelings today: where we make decisions based on our mind, will, and emotions, instead of the Word of

God. Nevertheless, we are not perfect, and when we miss the mark, thank God we can correct our mistakes, learn from our mistakes, and confess our sin to God. He will forgive us (1 John1:9).

When the first parents (Adam and Eve) to mankind sinned against God, He had a resolution: "And I will put enmity between thee and the woman, and between thy seed and her Seed; it shall bruise they head, and thou shalt bruise his heel" (Genesis 3:15). Women do not have seed; we carry it. In Genesis 3:15, God was talking about Jesus being the solution to restore mankind unto righteousness—the same Seed God foretold in Genesis 3:15, the same Seed prophesied in Isaiah 7:14, "Therefore the Lord himself shall give you a sign; Behold, a virgin shall conceive, and bear a son, and shall call him Immanuel (God with us)," the same Seed that the angel Gabriel prophesied, "The Holy Ghost (third person of the Godhead) shall come upon thee, and the power of the Highest shall overshadow thee: therefore also that holy thing which shall be born of thee shall be called the Son of God (second person of the Godhead) through the Virgin Mary (Luke 1:35; Luke 2:7) is the same Jesus available to us today.

If you have received Jesus as your Lord and Savior, know that you are able to move forward from any situation without feeling condemned. If you do not know Jesus, and you have made decisions based on your emotions, you can have a friend in Jesus. Never let a bad decision became a lifestyle. Receive Jesus today!

Salvation Confession (Romans 10:8–10, 13)

Father God, I confess with my mouth Jesus is Lord, and I believe in my heart that God raised Him from the dead. I repent of my sins by turning away from them. I receive your offer of forgiveness. Thank you, Jesus, for coming into my life. I am now clean and restored into righteous fellowship with you. Thank you, Jesus. I am now saved.

I know the example I used was small. Some of you who are reading this may have made a huge mistake that you feel you cannot recover from. Now that you have said the prayer of salvation, I encourage you to walk in the newness of life according to 2 Corinthians 5:17: "Therefore if any man be in Christ, he is a new creature: old things are passed away; behold, all things are become new."

Once you received Jesus as an offering for your sins, you are clean in the sight of God. Now when God looks at you, He sees Jesus's atonement for your sins. He sees you through the blood of Jesus. As a child of God, when the enemy tries to condemn you, know that when God takes notice of you, He does not see you for what you have done; He sees you and take into an account what Jesus did for you. So forgive yourself and live blessed.

Rededication Confession

"If we confess our sins, he is faithful and just to forgive us our sins, and to cleanse us from all unrighteousness" (1 John 1:9)

Father God, I have sinned against You. I (identify and acknowledge your sins here). I believe I am forgiven according to your Word. I turn away from _____ by not committing those sins again. Dear, Father, your Word says greater are you in me than he that is in the world, so I lean on your strength to live a righteous and holy life acceptable to you. Please remove those desires that is not of you. I give you free reign to replace those people in my life with a godly circle. Help me conform my mind to your ways instead of the world's way. In Jesus's name, amen.

Even saved people filled with the Holy Ghost miss the mark sometimes. Proverbs 22:6 says, "Train up a child in the way he should go: and when he is old, he will not depart from it."

You may be reading this book and believe you have fallen away from God; the good thing is you can always come back to God. For you to have once believed in God means you have some knowledge of God's expectation of you. Don't allow your past to hinder your future. You confessed your sins, and now you are back in fellowship with God. Like the prodigal son, you are accepted in God's family. Now do what is right in the sight of God and live blessed.

DAY 20

Believe You Have What You Prayed For

Have faith in God... Therefore I say unto you,
What thing so ever ye desire when ye pray, believe that
ye receive them, and ye shall have them.

—Mark 11:22, 24

Today I believe for the storm to stop and for healing. God made good on His word. I woke up this morning to the sound of rain beating on my window. The time is 4:00 a.m.; I thank God for waking me up to spend time with Him. I prayed; I wrote in my journal, and I just laid in my bed contemplating if I should call off work. I looked at the weather app on my phone, and it showed that it will be raining all day and some thunder. I thought about reasons to not drive in the rain, then I thought about reasons I should go to work. There are times when I get stuck on what to do trying to find signs to do something. In the Old Testament, God led His people with fleece and signs. Not saying that God would not lead with signs now... I mean He is GOD and could do whatever He wants. However, as born-again believers, filled with the Holy Spirit, God wants us to be led in this world not by signs but by His Word and Spirit.

As I laid in bed trying to figure out what to do, my soul and body wanted to stay in bed, but my spirit is moved by faith, which is not moved by the rain. Holy Spirit checked me and said just make a choice. If I do not go to work, I have the time to use to call off, and if I decided to go to work, I can pray the rain away; you know, name it and claim it. My God will protect me and not allow me to get wet. When it comes to storms, my spirit is build up to speak the storm away because so many times, I have heard rumors of storms occurring when I had things to do, and God always seems to stop the rain during my travel or allowed it to pass before I had something to do.

Let me just speak about this "name it and claim it" affirmation. There are a lot of people who have something against this affirmation. They believe that this "name it and claim it" is some hocus-pocus jargon where you get what you want by claiming it. Jesus spoke only what the Father gave Him to speak, thus He was able to have and do whatever He spoke because it aligned with what the Father told him. It is the same with us. Remember, we are created in the image and likeness of God; when we accepted the death, burial, and resurrection of Jesus for the remission of our sins, we became children of God, and the Holy Spirit came to take residence in us. Therefore, as long as you are "naming and claiming" what the Holy Spirit has given you to speak out loud from the Father, you shall have what you ask for.

I decided to act on faith and go to work. I decided to trust God and not be moved by what I saw in the physical. And you know what? When I went to work, the weather was not as bad as the early rain nor as bad as the weather app reported. Now I am not saying that we should not listen to the meteorologist. I believe we should be aware of our surroundings. What I am saying is that we should not allow what we see or hear deter us from what we believe God wants us to do in life. Have faith.

The Holy Spirit that lives in you is smarter than you and can see further than what you can see. Follow peace. As children of God, we are created in His image and likeness. We have the same creative abilities with our words that God had when He created the world. When you are presented with a situation, instead of acting on it, consult with God first in prayer. Tell Him what your heart's desire is, and if there are any obstacles, pray to Him about it. And if God tells you to move, do it despite how the situation looks. If God tells you to act, then have confident that He has made provisions for you.

What is it you believe that God is telling you to do?

Are your desires the will of God according to the Word of God?

What are some of the obstacles you see that appears to be standing in your way?

Have you taken those obstacles to God in prayer?

Solutions…

Write the solutions and act on the solutions step-by-step.

1) _____
2) _____
3) _____

As God gives you the solutions, continue to act until you achieve what God has placed in your heart. Be blessed.

Day 21

Every Good Thing Comes from God

*Every good gift and every perfect gift is from above, and
cometh down from the Father of lights, with whom
is no variableness, neither shadow of turning.*
—James 1:17

Today was a good day. Every day is a good day when I accomplished what I set out to do within a day. With all the news on sickness and death, my initial thought is to panic. Sometimes when you hear bad news, you just want to be around the people or things that will bring you comfort. No matter what day you are having, always remember that God is good. Everything good comes from Him. Even when you have bad moments or days where you are filled with sadness, never allow negative emotions to consume your heart where you cannot see the goodness of God. Perhaps when something bad happens, you may not be able to see the good thing in that moment, but when you reflect on the day, always try to find something good and build on it.

When you believe that God loves you, you know that He wants good things for you. Thus, when bad things happen to you, know that God will turn it for your good because He loves you. Satan comes to kill, steal, and destroy; therefore, if he is attacking you, settle in your mind that whatever Satan is trying to use to destroy you, his ultimate goal is to keep you from the plans that God has for you.

I know that God has a perfect plan for my life. I remember when I first got the news that my cousin was shot. I felt hopeless. The next day, I did not want to even talk to God. If I would have allowed that seed of bitterness and hopelessness to grow, I probably would have walked away from God. Thank God I know enough to know that God is not my enemy; you see, whatever is in you will come out under pressure, so get to know God now. I know God loves me, and when Satan tried to attack my faith, I was able to repent for my anger and get right back in fellowship with God.

Every good thing comes from God. Even when you cannot feel Him but your needs are met, give glory to God. Like in the book of Esther, God's name is mentioned in that story not a single time, yet you can see that God is moving in the lives of His people. You may not feel Him, He may not give you a word, but if you get to know Him, you will be able to recognize Him and give Him glory no matter what situation you are in.

DAY 22

─── ❧ ───

When God Makes Your Schedule

And we know that all things work together
for good to them that love God, to them who are
called according to His purpose.

—Romans 8:28

I once heard a pastor say she does not make her schedule, but her father makes her work schedule. That was such a revelation for me because despite the plans I have for my life, God has the final say. My confession became, "My Father makes my daily schedule." I have learned that if I keep God at the forefront of my life, no matter what happens, He is not surprised, thus He will work it out for my good.

Currently, I am a full-time employee and an online student. As I get further in my studies, my days are becoming cumbersome with the assignments and personal assignments that I believe God has placed on my heart to do. Each day, I am believing God to give me time and energy to do what each day requires of me. Therefore, I am more conscious of how many hours, which causes me to be selective, in what I give myself time to do. There are things that I have to say no to if I want to complete my personal assignments. When you know why you are doing something, it makes it easy to turn people down.

God is personable, and He cares for the things you are concerned about. That is why the Bible says to "cast your cares upon the

Lord for he careth…" God cares about your day even to the littlest thing. When you go to God in prayer, He will give you answers. You just have to be open to hearing Him and making the necessary changes He tells you to make in your life.

Even in times like this, the state is not fully open, which means minimum distractions from society. I can be bitter about how I cannot go to the places I want to go. I could even distract myself with social media and television…or I can recognize that all things work for my good and look for the opportunities that God is making available to me during the shutdown.

Our mind is so powerful that if we focus on God being good and working for our good, we are able to see how even in a negative situation God has a "ram in the bush" and "parting the sea" type of solution. Try Him! "Oh, taste and see that the LORD *is* good; Blessed *is* the man *who* trusts in Him!" (Psalm 34:8 NKJV). Trust God with your life, and allow Him to plan your day. What I mean by that is trust God when the unexpected happens. Whether it's good or bad, trust that He has you in the palm of His hands. He sees all, knows all, and has a plan for every situation; trust Him.

DAY 23

Stay Focused

And while they went to buy, the bridegroom came; and they that were ready went in with him to the marriage: and the door was shut.
—Matthew 25:10

We all want to be invited to something great and be a part of something great, but how many of us are ready to be great? It is easy to want than it is to be, easier to hope than to act on faith. Many of us are not where we want to be because when the time present itself, we are not ready. We get lost in the dream that we fail to prepare for the dream coming true. I want God to use me, but I understand that there are things in me that needs to be purified and refined before I enter what God has for me. God is a loving God. He will not set us up to fail. He rather take the time to prepare us for the call.

Today I had somewhere important I needed to be, and I almost missed my assignment by engaging in a frivolous conversation with my sister. I love my sister so much, and we have the best conversations that when it starts, we can talk for hours. I tried to time our conversation, allocating enough time to leave the house. When I finally got on the road, there was a detour, and I ended up at my destination later than expected. Holy Spirit, of course, checked me, and I was convicted. The enemy tried to condemn me, and for a second, I almost fell for it.

However, when you show up to work, it is not the time to have pity on yourself. No, when you show up, you either be ready or get ready. It is always better to be ready, but if you show up and you have to get ready, you give it your best. Feeling sorry for yourself during the time you are needed will only make the situation worst. Feel pity afterward, and do better next time. My church motto when it comes to being punctual is, "To be early is to be on time; to be on time is to be late." I had become comfortable being late and not being checked that I convinced myself it was acceptable as long as I was there before production began. I was so use to arriving later than expected and have my station completed that I expected it to be done when I arrived. However, this day was different. My station was not ready. I was disappointed, and my flesh wanted to blame someone, but the truth of the matter was that there was no one to blame besides me. If I was at my station early, I would have had time to get my station together.

In reference to the scripture above, there were ten virgins waiting to enter the banquet. Although all ten virgins showed up, only five were ready. The five that were not ready were not prepared for the night, and that unpreparedness caused them to be shut out of the banquet. Likewise, although I showed up, my tardiness prevented me from preparing for my responsibilities. I believe God warns before destruction, and since I was convicted by my actions, that was my warning. If I fail to take heed to that warning, I could find myself missing out on something great that God wants to do for my life. Unfortunately for the five virgins, they missed out on a great opportunity. Don't let that be you.

I used to think that all I had to do was show up. As I matured, I recognize that it is better to show up ready. I remember when I was working at a restaurant and we had some people to stay behind to help out. One of the people was goofing off. I remembered confronting his behavior, and the manager confronted me saying I should be happy he stayed behind to help. I felt bad for confronting the other person at that time. However, when I reflect on that day, I believe I was not wrong. If you are going to show up, then that means you have assigned yourself to work. What is the point of showing up if you are not prepared to do what is required of you?

It seems like people get used to quantity over quality. I submit this to you. Promotion comes from God even when He uses people to promote us. God is watching. If showing up and being unprepared did not work for the five virgins in the parable Jesus gave to his disciples, it will not work for us either. If you are going to show up, be prepared. In the words of Andy Mileo, "if you stay ready, you don't have to get ready."

DAY 24

— ⚬ —

What Are You Thinking?

*For God hath not given us the spirit of fear; but of
power, and of love, and of a sound mind.*
—1 Timothy1:7

A sound mind is to have self-control by not allowing your thoughts to rule your body or behavior. In social work, there is a model called the "Cognitive Triangle of Life," and it illustrates how what you think on, control your emotions, and your emotions will control your actions, and your actions (good or bad) will reflect those emotions (positive or negative).

Today I was awaiting my time to give my Zoom presentation. My appointment time was at 8:30 a.m. When 8:15 a.m. arrived, I prepared myself mentally to deliver the message. When 8:30 a.m. came, I was ready; when 8:35 a.m. passed, I thought perhaps the person before me was going over time. I decided to send an email to the facilitator letting her know that I arrived on time and that I was waiting to present. When 8:40 a.m. arrived, I began to worry and doubt myself.

Past thoughts of me making mistakes, not being prepared, and messing things up started to flood my mind. *Did I log in correctly? Am I on the correct site? What if I get a bad grade for not being present?* Then at 8:50 a.m., I became angry and accusative. I had experienced people in authority not liking me, looking over me, and I thought that my facilitator was doing the same thing. I was in the midst of writing another email when God stepped in… A response from the facilitator popped up in my email to explain that there was a mishap on her part; she did not schedule me for today, so she scheduled me for another day.

I heard someone say in a movie that "time is the revealer of all." Phraseology such as *that remains to be seen, patience is virtuous, reaping what you sow* all deal with allowing time to show the manifestation of a person's heart or the outcome of a situation. Too many of us are quick to react based on what we think and how we feel that we find ourselves or cause ourselves to relive our past experience by bringing past experiences into our future. We believe that people are against us because of some poor choices people in power have made against us in the past. Our thought life is the head of everything that follows.

In Deuteronomy 28:13, God said He "shall make thee the head, and not the tail; and thou shalt be above only, and thou shalt not be beneath; if that thou hearken unto the commandments of the LORD thy God, which I command thee this day, to observe and to do *them*…" That word *head* in the Hebrew is *Rosh* which means "ruler." God is able to place us in high places; however, how we respond to unfavorable situations will either position us to take our place in what God has caused us to do or cause us to be the tail being led by our emotions.

It is better to check the narrative you tell yourself while it is a thought than to allow a negative picture induce negative feeling to which you will act on. Having patience is one of the fruits of the Spirit, and if you grab ahold of patience, it will prevent you from acting out of anxiety and frustration. Sometimes, you have to see a situation through before making a judgment on it.

In 1 Samuel 10:8, the prophet Samuel instructed Saul to go to Gilgal before him and wait seven days until he meets him in Gilgal in order to offer burnt offerings and sacrifices of peace offerings. At that appointed time, Samuel would tell Saul what to do next. However, in 1 Samuel 13:8–10, it says,

> Saul tarried seven days, according to the set time that Samuel had appointed: but Samuel

> came not to Gilgal; and the people were scattered from him. And Saul said, Bring hither a burnt offering to me, and peace offering. And he offered the burnt offering. And it came to pass, that as soon as he had made an end of offering the burnt offering, behold Samuel came.

Saul allowed how the situation looked caused him to get out of the will of God. It was the seventh day, and instead of Saul waiting the whole day, he allowed what the situation looked like—people scattering from him, Samuel not being there, and the enemy gathering around him—caused him to go against the plan.

In life, things may appear opposite to how you expect it, but if you continue to ponder on how the situation looks, it will cause you to create thoughts that will ascribe to a negative narrative which will cause you to feel a negative way and have you respond in a way that can take you out of the will of God. Even if God wants to elevate you, that elevation is not automatic. Elevation comes from the Lord, but you have to be responsible in positioning yourself to rise. God chose Saul to be king, but it was Saul's behavior that placed him out of the will of God for his life.

Remember, your actions are a by-product of your thoughts. Good thoughts create positive responses; negative thoughts create emotional responses that usually lead to bad results.

Are you living life repeating old habits and getting the same old results? Perhaps you are in an unhealthy relationship, and you are wondering why do you keep falling for the same person? I encourage you to evaluate your thoughts.

What are you thinking on that gives you permission to enter into an unhealthy relationship?

What are you thinking that's causing you to respond in a negative manner?

What are you thinking on that prevents you to speak when you shouldn't be silent, overreact when you should give people the benefit of the doubt?

When you gain control of your thought life, your emotions and actions will follow. Majority of us are living the life we think we deserve. If you want better, then think differently.

DAY 25

―――― ⌒∿⌒ ――――

Don't Be So Quick to Take Ownership

*He that answereth a matter before he heareth
it, it is folly and shame unto him.*
—Proverb 28:13

I have a niece who, when she was younger, would always admit to things that she did not do. For example, if someone asked whose shoes are in the living room, she would respond "mine" without seeing whose shoes were in question, later to find out they were not hers. Or someone would ask, where is the remote control, and she would respond, "I know," and she would not know where it was.

How many of us are guilty of responding to a situation before knowing the whole story? Some of us answer a matter before hearing the whole story because we presume we know what the other person is going to say; sometimes we do it because we presume we know the situation. Some of us answer a matter before hearing it to dismiss the person or situation; you know, telling a person what they want to hear—"yeah, okay" or "blah blah"—so they can leave you alone. But God says to answer a matter before hearing or knowing the entire story from beginning to end will bring shame on us.

Today I was in the grocery store with my sister. We were in the self-service lane. I was at one register, and she was at the one next to me. When she left that register, the attendant asked me if I was at that register; knowing that my sister was at that register, I said yes.

I assumed that my sister called for help at the register. Once the attendant resolved the issue at the register, my sister heard me say I was at that register, and she asked me why I said that. I told her because I saw her at the register and assumed the attendant was there for her. My sister said to me, "You need to stop that (referring to me admitting something that I did not do). I did not use that register because it was broke." Thank God, nothing serious arose out of that situation.

As an afterthought, I pondered on what could have happened if the situation would have turned for the worst. What if the attendant was trying to see who broke the machine, and when I falsely admitted to being at that machine, I would have accepted responsibility for an act that did not concern me nor did I commit. I would have trapped myself in a situation that could have had negative consequences.

There is a story in the Bible of a man whose response caused him his life. When you answer a matter prior to knowing the truth, you can find yourself in a situation where your character is questioned. You can be seen as a liar. In 1 Samuel 31, Saul killed himself to avoid being captured by his enemies. However, a young man apparently knowing the discourse between David and Saul decided to falsely claim he killed King Saul expecting David to be pleased and reward him. However, the young man admitting to something he did not do caused him his life.

The Bible says in Proverbs 6:2 that "thou art snared with the words of thy mouth, thou art taken with the words of thy mouth." The word *snared* in the Hebrew is *yaqosh*, which means "fowler." According to Google, a fowler is hunting, shooting, or trapping of a wildfowl. The word *taken* in the Hebrew is *lakad*, which means "to catch in a net, trap, or pit." The Word of God is warning us to not allow our words to trap us.

So before you eagerly chime in, hear the whole story. Even if you have to ask questions, get the whole story before giving an answer. You might save yourself from having to retract your answer.

DAY 26

God Gives Good Gifts

*If ye then, being evil, know how to give good gifts unto
your children: how much more shall your heavenly
Father give the Holy Spirit to them that ask him?*
—Luke 11:13

My niece's birthday

Today's weather forecast was supposed to be raining and isolated storms. The plan for today was to celebrate my niece's birthday at the zoo; however, because of the bad weather report, we had a backyard party. My niece's only desire was to have dogs at her party. The family did not plan for this, but glory to God, it all worked out for my niece's desire; the family brought their dogs, and my niece ended her night saying this was the "best day ever."

God gives good gifts. In this scripture, the good gift that is being talked about is the Holy Spirit. I like how the Gospel of Luke compares God to our natural parents. If you being evil—that word in the Greek is *poneros* it means "evil in effect, corrupt, or sinner"— know how to give good gifts to your children, then OF COURSE God is able to give you what you ask for. God wants us to have a good life. He wants you to be full of joy. You just have to trust Him. What I love about my niece getting the birthday she wanted was that it came effortless. She only spoke what her desire was, and God orchestrated it. See, God even cares about the little things. We have to learn how to trust Him, and with trust comes patience, being able to wait on God and His timing.

There are some gifts that comes immediately, and there are some gifts we have to position ourselves to receive. God has not forgotten about you. He knows what your needs are.

Luke 11:9–13 states,

> And I say unto you, Ask, and it shall be given you; seek, and ye shall find; knock, and it shall be opened unto you. For every one that asketh receiveth; and he that seeketh findeth; and to him that knocketh it shall be opened. If a son shall ask bread of any of you that is a father, will he give him a stone? or if he ask a fish, will he for a fish give him a serpent? Or if he shall ask an egg, will he offer him a scorpion? If ye then, being evil, know how to give good gifts unto your children: how much more shall your heavenly Father give the Holy Spirit to them that ask him?

Ask, seek, and knock…taste and see that the Lord is good. What is in your heart? What is it that you want? Ask God for it. He hears you. Now are you willing to hear the answer? There are a lot of things I want, and in God's response, I either had to wait on it or position myself for it. Now understand this, God will not go against His Word, so check your heart. In James 4:1–3, it says, "From whence come wars and fighting among you? come they not hence, even of your lusts that Ye lust, and have not: ye kill, and desire to have, and cannot obtain: ye fight and war, yet ye have not, **Ye ask, and receive not, because ye ask amiss**, that ye may consume it upon your lusts." God's will is to give you the desires of your heart, according to His Word. He knows you better than you know yourself.

I desire marriage; I want to do life with someone. However, there are times, when I ask for a man, God will give me assignments like going to ministry school or getting more involved in church.

Initially, I would think perhaps God is positioning me to receive my man! But something interesting would happen...the desire for a man would disappear. When I was busy for the Lord, the thought of having a man during this time in my life seemed like an inconvenience. I am not saying that God will not position us to meet that special someone. However, I am saying that in that season of my life, God knew that even though I was asking for a man, what I really was asking was for validation and purpose. I received exactly what I needed when I served God: validation and purpose. Therefore, ask God for what you want and receive the answer.

That word *seek* in the Greek is *zeteo*, and it means "a search for something hidden." When I think of seeking something I want, I think about a scavenger hunt. A scavenger hunt is a game where the participants seek out things to find on a list. Only those who want what is on the list will participate. Are you willing to seek out what you are looking for? In Luke 8:17, it says, "For nothing is secret, that shall be made manifest; neither anything hid, that shall not be known and come abroad." In James 4:8, it says, "Draw nigh to God, and he will draw nigh to you." God created you, which means He knows you better than you. If you draw closer to God, He will come closer to you, and you will begin to know the fullness of Him and the gifts He has for you.

I believe one of the reasons my niece was able to end her day saying that her birthday was the "best ever" was because she recognized the manifestation of her desire based on what she sought in her heart.

Lastly, the Greek word for *knock* is *krouo*, it means "to rap, as in repeatedly pounding onto something." In Revelation 3:20, Jesus said, "Behold, I stand at the door, and knock: if any man hear my voice, and open the door, I will sup with him, and he with Me." When you are knocking at the door, you are making your presence known to the one on the other side. When you come to God in prayer, He listening to you is like Him inviting you to come in. God wants to do good to you not only because He is God but also because He is a loving Father.

My niece could have had an attitude and decided not to come to her party because initially during the planning process, it did not look the way she wanted it. However, because she showed up and made her presence known, she was able to reap the joy of her party by showing up. Have you made yourself available to God, or have you turned away because the initial process did not look the way you wanted it? God wants to give you the desire of your heart according to His will.

Now with all the wanting you desire, don't forget to receive God's greatest gift: Jesus, His Son, the second person of the Godhead. And God wants to give you above all you can ask or think of, and that is another great gift: the Holy Spirit. He is the third person of the Godhead. God wants you to have a full life. Part of having a full life is doing what God has called you to do, and that is to be a witness onto Him. Receive the Holy Spirit which is that power that comes upon you to be an effective witness for Christ. You are qualified for this gift because you have received Jesus as your Lord and Savior by confessing with your mouth and believing in your heart that God raised Him from the dead for the remission of your sins and is alive now.

Remember, Luke 11:13 stated if you can give good gifts to those who asked you, certainly God can give you the Holy Spirit. Just ask. You shall have what you ask for.

Pray this…

Dear Heavenly Father, I come to you today to ask for the Holy Spirit. Your Word says as your child who have received Jesus as my Lord and Savior that I am qualified to receive this gift. So I ask, give me the gift of the Holy Spirit. I believe I have the gift of the Holy Spirt right now, and as an act of my faith, I will speak what the Spirit has given me to speak. In Jesus's name, amen. (Take a deep breath, and allow what's in your spirit flow from your mouth.)

You have now the Bible evidence of speaking in tongues! Congratulations!

For more information on the Holy Spirit, read these scriptures:

John 14:16–17—Jesus promising that when He ascends into heaven, God will send down the Holy Spirit.

Luke 24:49—Jesus commissioning His disciples to wait for the Holy Spirit.

Acts 2:1–4—How the Holy Spirit fell on everyone despite their race or ethnicity.

Acts 10:38—Qualifications for the Holy Spirit

Acts 1:8—The power and purpose of the Holy Spirit

1 Corinthians 14:2—Holy Spirt, your heavenly language

DAY 27

———— ❧ ————

Inordinate Affection

I charge you, O daughters of Jerusalem, that ye stir
not up, nor awake my love, until he please.
—Song of Solomon 8:4

I love him. He loves me not. I love her. She loves me not. Why do some of us come to encounter people we want to be with yet do not want to be with us. To have companionship when I was in the world seemed easy yet resulted in tears and self-loathing. Now I am saved, and having companionship seems difficult, yet I don't feel like I have to lose myself in order to gain someone. The only person I want to lose myself to is Jesus. But when you really think about it, when you accept Jesus as your Lord and Savior, you find yourself—your true self, that wonderfully and fearfully created image and likeness of God's character self.

I love being me. Whenever I can look in the mirror and see beauty, I thank God because there was a time when I looked in the mirror and it felt like a stranger was looking at me. I thank God for Jesus and the plans for my life. However, when it comes to my heart's desire for a mate, my patience is tried.

I remember years ago, I was reading Colossians 3, and I came across verse 5 that read, "Mortify therefore your members which are upon the earth; fornication, uncleanness, inordinate affection…" Verse 6 says, "For such things' sake the wrath of God cometh on the children of disobedience..." Verse 10 states, "And put on the new man, which is renewed in knowledge after the image of him that created him..." I was curious in what inordinate affection meant in the Bible because when I read this, I was experiencing some inordinate affections that was affecting my thought life and mood. I was into someone who was not into me.

According to the *Strong's Concordance*, the word *inordinate* in the Greek is *pathos*, and it means "suffering passion, lust." I was suffering internally, and these feelings felt out of order. When you are out of order or out of the will of God, you will know it by your thoughts and actions. The Bible says there is a way that seems right unto a man but leads to death. I began trying to get his attention by making a complete fool of myself. I had experienced so many bad relationships that he just seemed so fresh and innovating that I wanted him. I would see him from time to time thinking it was God placing me in his presence. He would greet me from time to time, and in my mind, I was planning our wedding.

It began to weigh on my mind emotionally when my idea of him did not match what I was seeing in the natural. In my mind, he wanted me, but in reality, he was not interested. I began to be hurt by his presence when he spoke to other women. I felt rejected. When he gave other women hugs and gave me a nod or a side hug, I was hurt. When I spoke to him and he responded by calling me "hey you," I was heartbroken. The hurt I felt from a person who was a stranger in reality was affecting me emotionally, physically, and spiritually.

Then one day, I was reading the Bible, and I came across a scripture in Songs of Solomon: "I charge you, O daughters of Jerusalem, that ye stir not up, nor awake my love, until he please." The problem was I STIRRED UP SOMETHING that was not supposed to happen unless he pleased. The Hebrew word for *stir* is *uwr*. It means "to wake." The Hebrew word for *please* is *chaphets*. It means "to incline, to bend." I allowed my imagination to create a world that awaken a desire to a person who did not give me permission to have him. Everything was one-sided. You may be asking yourself, *How do I know when to awaken the love or if he pleases?* The answer is you two would be on the same page. The affection would be two-way rather than one-way.

You both would show mutual interest. Remember, God is not the author of confusion. If you have to wonder if someone like you, then hold off creating a fantasy that will attach you to a person who is either unsure or not interested.

I rationalize maybe he is shy; maybe he likes me, but the time is not right, maybe, maybe, maybe. Who wants a relationship based on maybes and what-ifs? I know I don't. My fear...I know God has not given us a spirit of fear...but my concern based on past experience was that one day, he would like me. From past experience, I usually ended up with my crush. What if this was the same thing? I did not want to be in another relationship when he finally realize he likes me. I did not want to be haunted with the thoughts of "what ifs." One day, I was talking to a lady about a relationship, and she said something powerful. She said she had an incident where the guy she liked did not like her until she was in a relationship. She said to him that he had his chance, perhaps he could try again if she becomes available. That guy never got a chance because she is now married.

Many of us are tried when it comes to the matter of our heart. We are on fire for God, but when it comes to waiting on God for a mate, that's where we are tested. We have to learn how to trust God with our heart. If the one we like is for us, it will work itself out. If he or she is not showing interest at this time for whatever reason, leave the situation in God's hand, and you finish doing what God has placed in your heart to do. (I AM SURE GOD IS NOT PUTTING IN YOUR HEART TO STALK OR TRY TO MAKE YOURSELF A PRIORITY IN SOMEONE'S LIFE.) I doubt you will be happy in the long run if you end up with someone because they did not want to hurt your feelings.

I do not have a remedy to help you get someone out of your heart or mind. I know it is hard to move one, especially if the person you want is in your presence, whether at work, church, class, etc. If you are like me, I will keep hope alive until he is with someone, or he just tells me he does not like me, or I am with someone else, or he does something that makes me see him as a donkey. I wished for me, it was that easy to stop liking someone who showed no interest in me. I understand that when you work closely with that person, every interaction is a sign of hope.

However, I will share with you how to maintain boundaries when it comes to crushing on someone who has not come around to liking you.

1) First, don't wake a desire in your mind or heart when the person has shown no interest. Remember, we are not in high school. Men are hunters and go after the one they want. I will caution you to be aware of good-looking men who are in need. It is better for a man to want you than to need you.

2) Let's say it's too late; you missed step one. Now you find yourself infatuated with someone who is not showing any interest in you, but you think he likes you. Until he comes to you and tell you he wants to get to know you, ignore all the double meaning signs such as him speaking to you, sharing some stories with you, giving you a dollar for the vending machine, touching your shoulders, or joking with you. Yes, these actions can be misinterpreted, but they also provide loopholes for him to deny he has feelings for you, especially if he has commitment issues or is not sure he wants to be with you. When he does nice things, thank him, but keep it moving. He tells a joke, laugh, but keep it moving. Do not build in your mind what is liable to crumble in your reality.

3) If you share with a close family or friend that you are crushing on this person and based on the story, your family or friend believes he likes you, too, and he is just shy. Until he tells you himself that he likes you and wants to be with you, treat him as another person.

4) Process your thoughts. This is something I constantly do when I find myself about to build on my fantasy relationship. I have to put our relationship into perspective. For example, if you work with your crush, and he calls you. Don't get excited yet. First, determine what is this phone call involving. If he only contacts you by phone when it is related to business or whatever project you two are involved

in, that is the indication of how he sees you. Perhaps he loves the value you bring to the team, but not for his life.

5) If you like someone in church…please process your thoughts and feelings about the situation. The church that I attend, if we work closely with each other, you may hear the words "I love you." Do not start planning the wedding. What he means is I love you in the Lord, or perhaps I love how your dedication to your role in Christ helps him do his responsibility effectively. You can acknowledge in your mind that hearing those words out of his mouth sound good, but do not read too much into it. Unless he tells you I love you, and I want to see more of you outside of whatever capacity you two work together, then just accept him as your brother in Christ.

6) Don't contact him. It is so tempting to rush things. You believe he likes you, or maybe you think he thinks you don't like him. You may have the urge to tell him how you feel. I don't know any movies or situations where telling a guy ended up with him realizing you were the one. What type of love story do you want to tell your kids? Dad was too scared to be rejected that Mommy stepped up and asked Dad to be with her. If he is not willing to go after the woman he wants to be with, what type of protector or provider will he be? Do you want to be the one having to push him? Supporting your man is good; pushing him when he needs to be pushed is good. But pushing him into a relationship with you…is not good. Don't be afraid to let go of the dream. God has someone who is willing to go after you and for you to receive.

7) Saving the best for last… In situations like this, Jesus will become your best friend. Cast your thoughts toward God because He hears and cares for you. He will give you the strength to put on a brave face each day. He will wipe your tears away. He will give you beauty for ashes. Trust Him. Know that time is on God's side. Who's for you is for you. One day, God may open the eyes of the one you like to see you, or in time, you may discover he is not what you really want in your life. Just trust God.

DAY 28

Will You Answer the Call from God?

And the Lord came and stood and
called as at other times, Samuel, Samuel. Then Samuel
answered, Speak for they servant health.
—1 Samuel 3:10

There are many who want to be called by God, but only a few will be chosen. There are many reasons why many want the call from God. There are some who wants the prestige, the fame; they believe it will financially prosper their life. Then there are others who have a heart to serve, compassion for the loss, or believe it's their call for duty. Nevertheless, only a few will be chosen.

The story of Samuel answering the call of God and the scripture from Matthew 22:14 saying "many are called, but few are chosen" came across my mind while I was watching TV. I had an unction to pray, but I did not want to turn away from the TV show. My rationale was it could wait because this show is almost over. I had an unction to pray in the spirit, so I spoke in tongues while watching TV. As I was praying in tongues, a stronger unction to pray appropriately checked me. The reason why I thought I could pray in the spirit and watch TV seemed crazy in retrospect. I thought, *Well I wouldn't understand what I am saying; God can use my body, but my eyes will be watching TV.* At that moment, it became a tug-of-war. My spirit was in conflict with my soul. I decided to yield to my spirit, turn away from the TV, and pray.

How many of us will admit that we want the call of God to be on our time and magnify us? Yet when God calls us, we tend to send Him to voicemail: *Leave a message at the sound of the beep, and I will return your call at my earliest convenience.*

What we really want is for God to tell us what He wants and let us decide if we want to do it. When I got the unction to pray, God did not tell me who or what I was praying on; He just wanted me to pray. When God calls you for an assignment, will you answer? Or do you want the details before you decide to commit?

Everyone wants to be lifted up until they find out what they have to do. In the text in 1 Samuel 3:10, God had previously called Samuel three times before he was instructed on how to answer. Now, there is no formula to answering God's call other than to obey what He tells you. However, Samuel did not know God; the prophet had to introduce him to God. When God called Samuel the final time, Samuel answered, and God told him the plan. After hearing the plan, it stated "…Samuel feared to show Eli the vision."

That word *feared* in the Hebrew is *Yare* (yaw-ray); it means "cause to frighten." Can you imagine having to tell the one who gave you shelter and cared for you that you were his replacement.

There is a difference between being called and being chosen. Just because you are called or invited to go somewhere or be something does not mean you have to answer or agree. However, when you are chosen or elected, that means you have positioned yourself to be selected. Although God called Samuel, God wasn't able to choose him or elect him until he positioned himself to be elected by directly answering God.

Too many of us are trying to live out the call on our life by trying to exclude God.

We want to be a wife but not let God choose our mate.

We want to be rich but not let God choose our career.

We want to do good works but glorify ourselves instead of using our good works to glorify God.

See, even though Samuel responded, "Here I am," he kept going to the wrong person. It wasn't until he identified that it was God who was calling him that he was able to be used for God's glory. The Bible says in Matthew 6:33, "Seek ye first the kingdom of God and his righteousness; and all these they shall be added unto you"—as a by-product of you serving God.

Remember, allow your good works to glorify God (Matthew 5:16).

Righteousness, *Dikaiosune*, means "an equity of character or act."

Put your trust in the Lord. When He calls, you answer Him. Get to know Him so you will be able to know His voice. It's like when someone calls you from an unknown number, you know not to answer because you are not familiar with that number. But if someone calls you with the right number, you will answer because you know that number. Get to know God.

DAY 29

—————— ✺ ——————

Cheering Others On

*But if you have bitter jealousy and selfish ambition in
your hearts, do not boast and be false to the truth.*

—James 3:14

Today is the day that I have been waiting for: I get to minister a sermon. In the Zoom class, there are three of us; the instructor asked who wanted to go first. Immediately, I volunteered to be first. It's best to go first, at least for me. It prevents me from comparing my sermons to others and being persuaded to change it. So I went first. I believe I did well. I got through the message, beginning and end.

Then it was time for the other two students to give their presentation. The second speaker was good, energetic. The third person was compassionate. My initial thought was jealousy. They were better than me. I, for a quick second, saw my brother and sister in Christ as competitors. Holy Spirit had to check me about my attitude. When I was able to check myself, I was able to support my brother and sister. You have to settle in your heart that what is for you is for you. No one can rob you of your position unless you give it to them.

How do you give up your position?

In the world, you compete for positions. The world makes you feel like there can only be one at the top. However, with God, who is rich, infinite, and author of creation, He never runs out of positions for you to serve Him. When I settled in my heart that we were on the same team, I was able to adjust my attitude for the better. Jesus said, "A house divided cannot stand." That is how it is in the body of Christ; even in the work field, when people are able to stay in their lane and work together, it makes it easy to complete the mission.

It is God who gives promotion, especially to His children. Even if you are not a child of God, just know that all things come from God, and the results are good.

DAY 30

━━━━━━━ ⌀ ━━━━━━━

Walk It Out

This I say then, Walk in the Spirit,
and ye shall not fulfill the lust of the flesh. For the flesh lusteth against
the flesh: and these are contrary the one to the other:
so that ye cannot do the things that ye would.
—Galatians 5:16–17

I left the house angry, and I arrived at my destination late. When I woke up in the morning, my day was planned. However, things are subject to change when you allow your feelings to consume you and let people get in your way. Growing up in my family, I have learned that people are subject to make you feel guilty if it gets them what they want. Even being a Christian, if you are not certain what it means to be a Christian, people will push their theory on you so they can get what they want from you.

In addition, if you don't control your emotions, those negative emotions can weigh you down which is why I was late to my destination. On the way there, I just kept replaying the incident in my mind and how it made me feel. When I arrived at my location, I was upset that I arrived tardy, then I started thinking about how my unpunctual behavior may seem to the others. To put icing on the cake, the station where I was responsible for was not organized, so I had to rush and interrupt other people at their position to help me with my work, which made me feel worst. Everything just appeared to get worse, and I became unfocused. I wanted to give up, but I was in the middle of production, so I just prayed that God would get me through this production.

What does it mean to "walk in the Spirit, and ye shall not fulfill the lust of the flesh?" There are some who believe walking in the Spirit is praying in the Spirit and being disconnected from the world. However, to walk in the Spirit means to operate from the fruit of the Spirit which is love, joy, peace, longsuffering (patience), gentleness (kindness), goodness, faith, meekness, and temperance (self-control) according to Galatians 5:22–23. The scenario I described previously was me yielding to the flesh. The works of the flesh according to Galatians 5:19–21 are adultery, fornication, uncleanness, lasciviousness, idolatry, witchcraft, hatred, variance (contention), emulations, wrath, strife, sedition, heresies, envying, murders, and drunkenness.

In regard to me, I was yielding to the works of contention. I was so consumed with the dispute that occurred earlier that I was allowing it to affect my work. In the Bible, when it comes to making an oath, it states, "But let your 'Yes' be 'Yes,' and your 'No,' 'No.' For whatever is more than these is from the evil one" (Matthew 5:37). I understand now how anything outside of yes or no can be from the evil one. The contention began due to someone asking me to do something. Instead of responding yes or no, I responded out of frustration because what was asked of me would interrupt what I had planned to do. Then I felt guilty on how I responded which just continued to weigh on me.

This is why it is important to know yourself and your reasons why you can do something or not. People may not accept the word no, but as long as you know your reasons why, you will not feel guilty for having to say no. As a matter of fact, most times, people can accept no; however, it is our past experiences that causes us to react to how we think they may feel. Remember, we are not mind readers, so we should not try to read other people's mind. Walk in the Spirit. If you find yourself in a situation, grab one or some of the fruit of the Spirit to help you respond in a godly manner.

If I could do a do-over, I would have operated out of self-control—self-control in my response and in my emotions. If I would have checked myself at that moment, I would not have allowed it to carry on once I removed myself from the situation. Thank God there is no condemnation in Christ. When I became too overwhelmed, I prayed to God. I casted my cares upon Him and allowed His strength to carry me. If He can do it for me, He can do it for you.

If you need a friend that is always there when you need him, call Him. If you do not know Jesus, I encourage you to get to know Him. God knew we would need a Big Brother in this world not only to save us from condemnation in hell's fire but also to give us an abundant life on earth.

Children of God, we are not perfect; we are still human, and we miss the mark sometimes. Nevertheless, the beauty of being a child of God is that you know how to make it right. As a child of God, when you received Jesus as your Lord and Savior, there was a miracle that took place in you where your spirit was recreated (2 Corinthians 5:17). You were made a new creature in Christ to where you were made able to walk in the image and likeness God intended you to do before the fall of man in the garden of Eden (Genesis 3). Hence, when you feel your flesh trying to take control in a situation, you are able to switch gears by choosing to operate in the Spirit.

If you are saved but you have fallen away from God, there is still hope for you. First John 1:9 says, "If we confess our sins, he is faithful and just to forgive us *our* sins, and to cleanse us from all unrighteousness."

Choose to walk in the Spirit.

DAY 31

Missing You (I Love You, Dee)

But I would not have you to be ignorant,
brethren, concerning them which are asleep,
that ye sorrow not, even as others which have no hope.
For if we believe that Jesus died and rose again, even so them
also which sleep in Jesus will God bring with them.
—1 Thessalonians 4:13–14

Today is my cousin's birthday. His life was stolen from us seven years ago. It's weird that every time this month, when it gets close to his birthday, I get emotional. It's not like I plan to think about him or that the month makes me sad. It's just in the month of my cousin's birth, it makes me realize what the devil stole from me, even my family. It is true, Satan comes to kill, steal and destroy. Thank God, He sent Jesus that we may have an abundant life.

Why do good people die, but the evil ones tend to live longer? I have many theories, but I rest knowing that God gave us His Word so we would not be ignorant. This scripture was given to me on October 1, 2013, by one of the church counselors. I remembered that morning I woke up and prepared to go to work. I wanted to pray, then I remembered I was angry. I said to God, *Why pray? My prayers didn't save my cousin.* I tossed my Bible to the side of me and laid back down. However, my spirit urged me to pick up the Bible and read from 2 Corinthians 5:8: "To be absent from the body, and to be present with the Lord."

I take comfort that my cousin is with the Lord, and that he is not in my past but is in my future.

The Word says, "But I would not have you to be ignorant, brethren, concerning them which are asleep, that ye sorrow not, even as others which have no hope. For if we believe that Jesus died and rose again, even so them also which sleep in Jesus will God bring with them." God does not want us to be in this world unaware about those who have died physically on earth. That is why He reminds us in His Word about those who "sleep in Jesus" or are saved; God will bring those who die on earth to be present with Jesus in heaven.

It is hard to handle when someone you love dies. Although we as Christians believe that there is life after death, we still hurt while we try to adjust to not seeing that person anymore. One can never prepare oneself emotionally to how you will handle a loved one's death. This year, 2020, when the thought that my mom was not going to be with me...I couldn't prepare for her not being here with me. However, if God sees fit to let us live another day, we have to find strength in Him to help us. It seems like nothing is new under the sun, but when you are able to look back and see how God brought you through a tough situation or you look at others and see the strength of God in them, you are encouraged to move forward.

The first death that I can remember to change the dynamic of my family was in 1993; my dear auntie died from breast cancer. I can remember where I was when my mom told me about the news. I remember the funeral; I remember the change the family went through trying to recover. Then we created a new normal. Twenty years later, in 2013, our family was hit with a hard blow when my cousin was murdered. It is still different, but I know from past experience, we will create a new normal to where our loved ones will continue to be with us in spirit until we are able to meet with them in heaven. I pray we all make it.

So if you have experienced a loss of a loved one, I cannot tell you how to grieve. However, I can encourage you to look forward because the past is a memory, but those who died in Christ, at the appointed time, will all be raised in Christ. God loves you and cares for you. If you ever needed a reason to draw on the strength of God, the time is now. Do not allow the death you experience to take away from the life God wants you to have. Remember, just a little while longer, you all will be together.

DAY 32

— ⸙ —

Race Wars

There is neither Jew nor Greek,
there is neither bond nor free, there is neither male nor
female: for ye are all one in Christ Jesus.
—Galatian 3:28

I'm convinced that God does not judge a matter the way we do as humans. God is smarter than us, and He knows the heart of man. However, sometimes we allow traditions and cultures to take away the beauty of God by allowing those differences to prevent coming together on what matters: our love for God. It just seems that politics and people wanting power have turned an experience with God to be a tug-of-war; each side is trying to prove that they are right. They forget that God never wanted us to convince people of who He is but love them, especially, if they are different. It is the goodness of God that brings people to repentance.

The most heated yet respectful conversation that I have ever had with someone was with someone who believed differently than me. Although I disagreed with what that person spoke, I left the conversation understanding why that person believed the way she did. When a person believes what they believe in, it is hard to change their mind, especially if they see the benefit in what they believe in. I did a lot of things that was against what I now believe, but through prayer and God's goodness, I was able to recognize the error of my ways and turn from those evil things and move forward with my relationship with God.

I was watching this movie tonight where two sides were fighting. Now, typically people tend to root for the underdog; however, in this movie, the underdog represented the opposite of what I believed in, yet on both sides, there were good and bad people. Therefore, instead of rooting for a particular group, I decided to root for good versus evil. The mission determined what was good versus evil.

Currently, it feels to me that we are in a climate where instead of choosing based on our shared phenotype, shared political party, and things on the surface, this season is causing us to look within our hearts—to recognize that there are good and evil on both sides, whether it is race, political party, etc.; if we only focus on the surface and only siding with people because they look like us or in the same group, it blurs our vision to measure good and evil. However, if we focus on the mission despite how different that person looks on the surface, we could learn to embrace our differences and work together on the mission.

You know, we can learn a lot about a person if we listen to them and watch their behavior. Although we cannot see the matters of a person's heart, God has given us tools to help us to connect with good people. The word says that out of the mouth flows the issues from the heart, and by a person's fruit, you will know them. God did not focus on race or ethnic group unless it was to describe a person's birthplace or culture. And if He told us to stay away from a particular group, it was because of their behavior or belief toward Him, not because of their physical makeup.

I found it interesting that God gave man dominion over everything except each other. Yet we try to dominate each other, not recognizing that we are operating out of the curse. Love, laugh, and live. Being a follower of Christ is not about what your political belief is or your race. No, it is the matter of your heart. Being a Christian is choosing in your heart that you believe Christ died for your sins and is risen, and you have made the decision to follow Him. Don't allow other people to rob you of your salvation just because you don't fit their mode of how a Christian should be. Let the Bible be your standard.

DAY 33

❦

Not by Sight

For we walk by faith, not by sight.
—2 Corinthians 5:7

I had the weirdest morning. I finally got up at 6:19 a.m. which was late for me considering 6:30 a.m. is my departure time from home. I was upset, but fortunately, I have gotten most of my things ready at 3:00 a.m. when I initially woke up. After my attempt to do something decent with my hair, I looked at the clock on the wall, and it was 7:27 a.m. I panicked! Now I will have to stay at work until 4:00 p.m. So I rushed out of the house trying to make it to work by 7:45 a.m. I got in the car, and the clock showed 7:12 a.m. Now, I am confused. Change of plans, now I'm trying to get to work by 7:30 a.m. so I can leave work at 7:45.

Later in the day, I was determined to make it to church on time. I was so disappointed in myself for not being ready when I arrived at church late that Sunday that I did not want to relive the agony of being unprepared. So I came home from work, made a quick snack, watched my favorite show, and was out of the house at 5:37 p.m. As I was driving on the freeway, I looked at my clock, and it was 5:09. Wow! What is really going on? It wasn't until later that I realized the satellite clock was showing the wrong time.

Many of us are guilty of reacting to a situation based on what was presented in front us. Sometimes what is in front of us is seen as facts or a lie. Sometimes what's in front of you can cause happiness or fear. However, no matter what is in front of you, stay focused on truth. The truth never changes even based on circumstances. For example, the truth is I love my nieces, and that doesn't change based on the fact that they can be annoying or crazy at times.

In the example I used about time, my behavior was based on the clock; because the clock was unstable, my behavior was unstable. I was tossed to and fro all because my clock was malfunctioning. But with God, you never have to wonder, you just trust Him, and keep it moving.

When you are led by your feelings and circumstances, there are times you will be up or down, and in the inside, it may feel like a whirlwind, and you may feel exhausted. In Philippians 4:11–13, it says,

> Not that I speak in respect of want: for I have learned, in whatsoever state I am, therewith to be content. I know both how to be abased, and I know how to abound: everywhere and in all things I am instructed both to be full and to be hungry, both to abound and to suffer need. I can do all things through Christ which strengtheneth me.

No matter what life throws at you, be at peace with God. Do what you know is right, and everything will fall into place.

In regard to my two examples, when I focused on the time, I was tossed to and fro; one minute I was rushing, the other minute, I was slowing down. But if I just would have done what I knew to do and that was to get ready and leave the house, it would not matter what the clock showed.

Part of this faith work is to walk with God. Trust Him and acknowledge Him in all we do (Proverb 3:5–6). Stop concerning yourself with the details. You want to get married, trust God to bring it to pass. You want a better job, trust God to bring it to pass. Psalm 37:25 states, "I was young and now old, yet I have never seen righteous forsaken or their children begging bread." No matter how the picture may look, trust God, and do what is expected of you, and you will overcome any obstacles. Remember, you can do all things through Christ who strengthens you.

DAY 34

——— ✺ ———

Reflection

*Ye shall know them by their fruits. Do men gather grapes
of thorns, or figs of thistles? Even so every good tree bringeth
forth good fruit; but a corrupt tree bringeth forth evil
fruit. A good tree cannot bring forth evil fruit, neither
can a corrupt tree bring forth good fruit. Every tree that
bringeth not forth good fruit is hewn down, and cast into
the fire. Wherefore by their fruits ye shall know them.*
—Matthew 7:16–20

As I am editing this book, God is still revealing things to me even through the process of completing this book. This was a difficult project only because it required discipline, which I lack. You can tell how someone is by watching their lifestyle. I even think about my weight; I am 10 lbs over which by medical statistic means I am obese. Why? Because I lack discipline. I digress.

For this entry, I want you to focus on you. I have learned that in this world, there is no competition for me but me. Each day, we have to be better than who we were yesterday. We all have so many different talents that if we tried to compete against each other, we might find ourselves losing ourselves. It doesn't matter how many people who are called to do what you do because only you will be able to reach people in the style that God has given you. So be you, and be the best you can be. So many times, I was discouraged writing this book focusing on other people that these scriptures reminded me that it is not about me. The work that I do is to glorify God who speaks to me.

In reading Ephesians 1, God reminded me that it is not about me. In verse 4, it says, "According as he hath chosen us in him before the foundation of the world, that we should be holy and without blame before him in love: Having predestinated us unto the adoption of children by Jesus Christ to himself, according to the good pleasure of his will…" God has chosen you before the world was created and predestinated you to be a part of His family as His child. The Greek word for *chosen* is *eklegomai*. It means "to select." The Greek word for *predestinated* is *proorizo*. It means "determine before." The path of good and evil was determined before you entered into this world. Therefore, if you stay on the good path, you will reap the rewards predestined for you to receive. In contrast, if you go on the evil path, you will reap the consequence for going in that direction. God has selected you, but the choice is still yours to accept.

After reading Ephesians 1:4–5, that led me to inquire about that scripture from the reference column which led me to read Romans 8:28: "And we know that all things work together for good to them that love God, to them who are the called according to his purpose." What a relief! We do not have to make things work out. God has a purpose that He wants to fulfill through you.

Lastly, I ended my reading with 2 Timothy 1:9: "Who hath saved us, and called us with an holy calling, not according to our works, but according to his own purpose and grace, which was given us in Christ Jesus before the world began…" When I read this, I felt like the weight was being lifted off my shoulder. We have gifts in us that God has placed for His glory. Although there are people who have chosen to use their God-given talent for evil, it doesn't take away that those gifts and talents are from the Lord. When He placed those gifts inside of you, He also had a purpose for you in Him.

Ever watch people sing, and you are so moved by their voice? You know they were destined to become a singer. Or a child who build things when he or she were little then grow up to be an engineer or architect? When we rise in position, it is not only according to our works but according to God's own purpose and grace.

I like what Paul said in 1 Corinthian 2:17: "For Christ sent me not to baptize, but to preach the gospel." Paul knew what he was called to do and did not allow distractions to prevent him from doing what God chose him to do. How many of us are caught up in peer pressure, being distracted by what others are doing that we fail to focus on what we are supposed to be doing in this world? Or we know what God has called us to do, but because of peer pressure and wanted to be validated by people, we act like Sarai and try to hurry the vision of the Lord in our life?

Take a page out of the lives of Joshua, David, and Paul; stop trying to make things happen and just position yourself to receive what God has for you. Joshua and Caleb positioned themselves to receive the promised land (Deuteronomy 1:36–38). David positioned himself to receive the crown by simply being faithful with the little things (1 Samuel 16:1), and Paul accepted the calling on his life and did not allow his past to prevent him from moving forward in Christ (Acts9:11–12).

If you do not know what God has called you to do, start with your talents; start by doing what you were created to do and that is to worship God. Jesus commissioned us to preach the gospel. The word *preach* in the Greek is *kerusso*. It means "to proclaim or publish." Use your talents to glorify God, whether it's in songs, novels, health care, environmental work, etc. Let your good work glorify God, and let Him promote you in His timing. In this season of your life, there are no competition against you but you. So be who God created you to be, and be the best at it.

DAY 35

— ✺ —

The Finish Line

I have fought the good fight, I have finished
the race, I have kept the faith.
—2 Timothy 4:7

It does not matter how you begin but how you finish. Paul was writing a letter to Timothy about his journey in preaching the gospel of Christ. He was talking about the good fight he endured for God's sake. Prior to being saved, Paul was an enemy of God. He persecuted the church and even took part in killing one of the disciples, Stephen. Paul started off as an enemy of God to become an adopted child of God and wrote two-thirds of the Bible.

Where are you in life? Are you happy or fulfilled? Remember, it is not too late to switch gears. Perhaps you are on the right path, but it just does not look how you envisioned. Don't give up, and stay the course. You have to fight for what you want because Satan is seeking whom he can devour. He is the father of lies, and he comes to steal, kill, and destroy, whether it's your life, your dreams, or you. You have to fight.

The word *fight* in 1 Timothy 6:12 is *agon,* and it means "a contest or effort or anxiety." Unlike the word *fight* in 2 Timothy 4:7, it is used to describe a struggle—to compete for a prize.

Today, I am on my last chapter, Day 35, of *Everyday Life is a Sermon.* I am excited to close this chapter of writing to my book. I am excited for the next chapter of what to do. However, it was definitely a fight to get from Day 1 to now. I had faith—the substance of things hoped for, the evidence of things not seen. To write this book was a battle in my mind and flesh. Daily were thoughts that I could not do this. In my flesh, there were times that I did not want to do this for whatever reason. But something in my spirit, perhaps Holy Spirit kept pulling me. The Holy Spirit in us wants us to accomplish the work of the Lord, and our flesh will find any reason not to.

I was put in a situation that when the Word of the Lord came to me, I had to act on it by putting it in this book instead of just thinking on it. There will always be an opportunity to pull back or even walk away from what God has called you to do, yet it is up to you to fight the good fight of faith.

It is finished!

THANK YOU!

— ❧ —

Thank you for purchasing this book. I pray this book was as encouraging to you as it was for me writing it. I pray that God has revealed some things in you to help your latter years be better than the former years. Every day, God is talking to us, but it is up to us to hear Him. Start paying attention to your day and see how God speaks to you. Read God's Word so you will be able to follow what He is saying. The scriptures I have used in this book, use them as guidelines to start reading the Bible. Get familiar with God's voice through the Holy Bible, and begin to experience God speaking to you daily.

Live blessed!

REFERENCES

The New Strong's Concordance
Holy Bible

ABOUT THE AUTHOR

Sierra Dunklin is a follower of Christ! As a Christian, she is spreading the good news of Christ in the capacity of writing, street ministry, and walking in love. Born and raised in Detroit, Michigan, she went through a lot of ups and downs to finally be in the position to where she obeyed God and walked in the calling on her life. In 2013, she was called to evangelize on a local scale in which she joined her church's outreach street ministry team. In 2014, God called her to go to ministry school, and she answered the call in 2019. She is currently in Pistis School of Ministry.

Sierra wants you to be encouraged, to step out in faith, and do what God has called you to do in life to leave your mark. Stop sitting on the sidelines and get in the game! Be blessed.

CPSIA information can be obtained
at www.ICGtesting.com
Printed in the USA
BVHW081141131021
618855BV00002B/212